THE BACK COUNTRY
HORSEMAN'S GUIDE

BRUCE KARTCHNER

TATE PUBLISHING, LLC

✤DEDICATION✤

To my wonderful and loving wife, Kathy, and to my family for allowing me the time to wander all over the beautiful state of Utah; and for all of the thousands of volunteers of Backcountry Horsemen of America, that have spent countless hours working to keep America's public lands and trails open for saddle stock use.

✯ACKNOWLEDGEMENTS✯

Dr. Bill Day, of Utah State University, was the inspiration for this trail guide. Bill and his family moved to Utah and looked for a trail guide to introduce them to Utah's public lands. Dr. Day proposed to Backcountry Horsemen of Utah that all of the chapters contribute a few of it's members favorite trails to a book, which could be sold as a means to raise funds to help keep trails open. Bill developed a portion of the format for this book. Several of the trails were taken from Dr. Day's original research. Thank you, Dr. Day, and to those Backcountry Horsemen of Utah that contributed trail descriptions for Dr. Day's original manuscript.

Steve Guymon, education chairman of Bridgerland Backcountry Horsemen, contributed "Using Horses on Utah's Public Lands." Steve is one of the original founding members of Bridgerland Backcountry Horsemen and has spent the past decade or more actively working on the process of keeping our public trails open for future generations.

The trail maps shown with each description were derived, with permission, from "National Geographic's" "TOPO!" Thank you, "National Geographic," for allowing me the use of these maps.

Portions of this book were taken from the "Leave No Trace" training manuscript.

UTAH BACKCOUNTRY AND URBAN HORSE TRAILS CONTENTS

Utah Backcountry and Urban Horse Trails at a Glance

8

FOREWORD

Riding a great horse (or mule!) on a gorgeous mountain trail at the peak of fall color is one of life's truly great pleasures. Utah is covered with a spider-web of excellent riding trails, with shutter-bug views, clear air, water, and sky. If you are looking at this book, you have probably already raised the dust on a few of these trails, perhaps even to the point of memorizing every twist and bend of your local trails, and are looking for a new vista to enjoy with your 4 and 2-legged riding companions. If so, then this book is definitely for you. Bruce Kartchner has done your trail homework for you. How do you get to the trailhead? Where do you park your rig? Can you take the whole scout troop? Is there water/bathroom/camping? What is the trail like? How steep? How long? Where is the map? Will there still be snow in May? Can Old Dobbin make it up? Will there be bicycles to spook my goofy young horse? And will there be a steep drop off for him to flee over the edge of if he does? And, just in case he does, what is the phone number of the local vet?

This book is destined to be dog-eared in many a Utah saddle bag, one of which will be mine. Taking this book along on your next trail ride will be almost as good as taking along the Back Country Horsemen (see WWW.BCHU.com). The book will show you the trail, but it won't cook you dinner. So buy the book, join BCHU, and be glad you are in Utah, where the trails lead you by still waters, through waist-high meadows of wildflowers, and to the craggy peaks where mountain goats scale tiny rock ledges (see "Timpanooke Trail").

Safe and Happy Trails,
Cindy Furse

✳PREFACE✳

Over the past 20 years, I have ridden in many of the public land areas of Utah's backcountry. I have experienced with my equine (and human) friends the wonderful diversity that can be enjoyed in the beautiful state of Utah. It is my hope that this guide to some of Utah's horse trails will give the reader as many fantastic experiences.

I am a longtime member of Backcountry Horsemen of Utah. This organization is dedicated to keeping trails, and access to public lands, open for all saddle stock users. Part of the proceeds of this trail guide will be donated to Backcountry Horsemen of Utah, and Backcountry Horsemen of America, to help in this effort. For more information about BCHU, visit their website: WWW.BCHU.com.

✳INTRODUCTION✳

Utah's diverse backcountry is truly remarkable–from high alpine meadows to the driest of desert terrain. Every trail that I have explored leads to a dozen more. One could spend a lifetime of exploration and never see all that Utah has to offer. Over 80% of Utah is public land; most of it is open to travel by horseback. There are 15 wilderness areas, numerous national parks, 43 state parks, millions of acres of national forest, and Bureau of Land Management property. Over 40 of these areas are in the nation's inventory of road-less areas.

The Wilderness Act of 1964 has protected many of these areas from further development and permanently sets them aside for preservation in their natural state. Ever changing regulations, by those agencies charged with the care of these lands, threaten to keep saddle stock from using these lands in the historical way that they have been used by saddle stock. It is my belief that we must monitor the public land regulations to keep this growing number of regulatory restrictions from keeping stock users from using public lands.

Many of the trails in Utah were established by wildlife, Native Americans, early American Calvary, ranchers, cowboys, and livestock. This guide explores some of the historical trails, as well as many modern-day, recently established routes. Some of the trails are remote and isolated, and offer solitude–a place where other travelers will rarely be seen. Other trails are very popular, with lots of traffic and plenty of opportunities to socialize with other users.

All stock users should practice "Leave No Trace" ethics in order protect the public resources.

If we do not take care of our public lands, our children and their children may not have the privilege to travel where our grandfathers have traveled.

LEAVE NO TRACE ETHICS

Plan Ahead: Take maps of the area and study the route to be taken. Check with the local land agency about regulations and restrictions, such as group size. Ask about feed and travel conditions for the area you will be traveling. When possible, avoid travel in high use areas. The old saying is that "if you do not like Utah's weather, wait five minutes and it will change." It is not unusual to have a sunny, mild morning turn into strong winds, turning to rain by noon and to snow by dark–just to do it all over again the next day. Go prepared when traveling Utah's backcountry.

Travel and camp on durable surfaces: Durable surfaces include established trails and campsites, rock, gravel, dry grasses, or snow. When tying up horses, never tie a horse to a tree for long periods of time. To contain stock, use a high line on a durable surface. Move the high line every few days, and clean up any manure and loose feed. Camp at least 200 feet from any water source.

Dispose of waste properly: Pack it in, pack it out. Dispose of solid human waste in cat holes at least 200 feet from water.

Leave what you find: Preserve the past. Examine but do not touch cultural or historic structures and artifacts. Do not build structures, furniture, or dig trenches.

Minimize Campfire Impacts: Campfires cause lasting impacts to the backcountry. Use a lightweight stove for cooking, and enjoy a lantern. Where fires are permitted, use established fire rings, fire pans, or mound fires.

Respect Wildlife: Observe from a distance. Do not follow or approach them. Protect wildlife and your food by storing rations and trash properly. Control pets at all times, or leave them at home.

Be considerate of other visitors: Respect other visitors and protect the quality of their experience. Be courteous. Yield to other users on the trail. Take breaks, and camp away from trails and other visitors.

RECOMMENDED EQUIPMENT FOR TRAVELING UTAH'S BACKCOUNTRY

Gear and Accessories:
Water–2 quarts to one Gallon.
Waterproof matches in a water proof container.
Fire starters.
First aid kit both for humans and horses.
Insect repellant for both humans and horses.
Sunglasses, sun block, and lip balms.
Pocket Knife, whistle, mirror, flashlight, compass.
Area map and guides.
Clothing:
Rain gear that can also be worn as wind protection.
Extra layers of shirts, coats, wool hat.
Gloves, warm and waterproof as well as functional for the current weather.
Wide brimmed hat to ward off sun and wet weather.
Food:
Always take more food than you will think you will need for the trip. If you are lost or forced to stay out over night you will be glad you thought ahead.
Other Items:
Hobbles, high line rope, lead rope.
Camera and film.
Snacks, pain reliever, other medicines.
Pliers, wire cutters, bailing wire or twine.
This guide is intended to be an overview of the routes and should be used for initial planning to the travel area. Careful study of topographical maps of the area can enhance

your experience and keep you safe. Prior and proper preparation should always be practiced before traveling any of these routes. The remoteness and isolation of some of the routes can cause trouble for the unprepared traveler. Traveling safely means being prepared and informed. The estimated miles and travel times that are listed with each route do not take into consideration different breeds of saddle stock and their rates of travel.

By using this guide, I/We recognize Utah State Law, UCA78–27b–Limitations on liabilities for Equine and Livestock Activities–and release the author and publisher from any responsibility due its use in planning or traveling in the areas described. Also, recognizing the fact that whenever saddle stock use is involved, there is a potential for injuries to horses/mules, riders and spectators; also recognizing that the author and publisher of this trail guide cannot know the condition of the trails or the experience of riders or saddle stock taking part in the trail ride.

UTAH BACKCOUNTRY AND URBAN HORSE ROUTES AT A GLANCE

Name of Trailhead	Type of Route	Travel Time	Estimated Miles
Horse Transfer Station-Mill/Tibble Fork	Loop	2.5	4.25
Horse Transfer Station-Box Elder	Loop	5.5	13
Horse Transfer Station-Mill/Mud Springs	Loop	3.5	7.5
Timpooneke Campground	Out and Back	6	12
Battle Creek	Loop	3.5	10.25
High line Trailhead	Out and Back	6	15
Settlement Canyon	Loop	3	9
Loop Campground	Out and Back	4	8.5
O.P. Miller Campground	Loop	4.5	9
Wrangler Trailhead, Dimple Dell	Loop	2	6.4
12300 S. 1000 West	Out and Back	2	4
Corner Canyon Road	Out and Back	5	14
Blackhawk Campground	Loop	3.5	10

Shingle Creek	Out and Back	5	11
East Fork-Bear River	Out and Back	5	17
Holbrook Canyon	Out and Back	3.5	8
Christmas Meadows	Out and Back	4.5	13
South Fork	Out and Back	5.5	12
Narrows West Trailhead	Out and Back	7	22
Corner Canyon Road	Out and Back	2	6
Antelope Island	Loop	3	9.5
The Post	Out and Back	9.5	23.5
West Fork–Black's Fork	Out and Back	5.5	15
Horseshoe Canyon	Out and Back	4	7
Crystal Lake Trailhead	Loop	6	17.7
Ledgefork at Smith & Morehouse	Out and Back	4	11
Dry Canyon Trailhead	Loop	3	5.5
Jordan Narrows	Out and Back	3	11.6
Spanish Valley Road	Out and Back	2.5	8
Wildlife Refuge	Loop	4	12.6
Loafer Mountain	Loop	4.5	9.5
Whiting Campground	Out and Back	3	7
Dewey Bridge - Colorado River	Loop	3	10

North of Snow Canyon	Loop	2.5	8
Corrals at Kodachrome Basin	Out and Back	4	14
Sandy Ranch	Loop	5	14
Yellow Pine Campground	Out and Back	3.5	7
Echo Reservoir	Out and Back	20	60
San Rafael Bridge Campground	Out and Back	20	7
Blue Hill	Loop	3	7
Bloody Hands Gap	Out and Back	3	8.5
Box Elder- Stansbury	Loop	4	15
Cottonwood Canyon	Loop	3	8
Fifths Water	Loop	3	8
Hamongog	Out and Back	5	14
Holt Canyon	Out and Back	5	20
Middle Fork	Out and Back	3.5	9
Seven Mile	Out and Back	4.5	8
Steel Hollow	Loop	4	10
Yellos Fork	Loop	3	7

UTAH BACKCOUNTRY AND URBAN HORSE TRAILS

BATTLE CREEK TRAIL, UTAH COUNTY

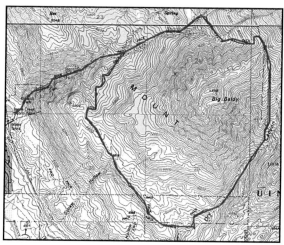

*Battle Creek is rugged and climbs fast along a creek
with some great views of a waterfall.*

Topo Map: Orem, # 40111-C6-TF-024
Name of Trailhead: Battle Creek
Name of Trail: Battle Creek Trail, Utah County
Trail #: 050
Property of: UNITED STATES FOREST SERVICE
Other Trails used by this route: Indian Trail - #049, Curley
    Springs Trail - #592
Connecting Trails: Great Western Trail
Directions from the closest town to trailhead: On the west
    side of Pleasant Grove from Utah Highway 89, turn
    east on 200 South Street. Travel east about 2.25 miles
    and the road will turn northeast past a debris basin
    reservoir. Parking is in the clearing at the end of the
    street, about 1/4 mile from the turn.
Road Conditions: The roads are all state, county, or locally
    maintained and should be in good condition year
    round.

Parking instructions: Parking is at the end of the highway, and it is a dispersed parking lot.

Parking capacity: 5 trucks and trailers

Direction of trail from parking area: The trail leaves the parking lot, east - northeast.

Elevation at T/H: 5200
Highest Elevation: 7300
Steepest Grade: 23%
GPS T/H Longitude: 111°42′ 4.84″ N
GPS T/H Latitude: 40°21′ 48.82″ W
Number of Feet Climbing: 4157

Camping and use restrictions at trailhead and along route: Water for Stock, Primitive Camping, Weed Free Hay, Dispersed Camping

Difficulty: Moderate

To complete this route, horses need to be: Moderately Fit

Trail Route & Directions: From the parking area, the trail travels east until it intersects the Indian trail. At the intersection follow the Indian Trail south to the Curley Spring Trail. Follow Curley Spring Trail back to the Battle Creek Trail.

General description of route: The trail starts climbing almost right out of the parking lot and continues to climb until it intersects the Indian Trail (in the basin below Timpanogas). The trail route is along the south-facing slope and some tree cover, but is usually in the open. It follows a steep ravine with some spectacular waterfalls. The east end is tree covered. There are many springs in the basin above that should offer plenty of stock water.

Type of Route: Loop

Length of Route in Miles: 10.25

Estimated travel time: 3.5 Hours

Route Attractions: Scenery, Conditioning, Drinking Water, Campsites, Cell Phone Accessible
**Normal Temperatures during
recommended months of use:
Spring:** Cool to Mild
Summer: Mild to Hot
Fall: Cool to Cold
Months of Accessibility: April to October

Predominant trail surface: Rock, Jeep Trail, Dirt, Loose Rock
Hazards: Rock Slides, Steep Sections of Trail, Narrow Trail with Steep Drop-offs
Description of Hazards: The south side of the Battle Creek trail drops off into a ravine with a stream generally running at the bottom. One area, about midway up the Battle Creek trail, snakes past a waterfall.

**Current Level Of Use:
(High - greater than 7 in group; Low - 3 or less.)
Horsemen:** Moderate
Motorized: None
Bicyclists: Seldom
Hikers: Moderate

Tack & Equipment Dealers: Am. Fork IFA Country Stores, 521 W 200 North, AMERICAN FORK, 84003, (801) 756–9604
Police: Utah County Sheriff, 3075 North Main, Spanish Fork, 84660, and (801) 851–4000
Veterinarian: South Valley Large Animal Clinic, 1791 W 11400 South, SOUTH JORDAN, 84095 (801) 254–2333
Hospitals: Utah Valley Regional MED Center, 1034 N 500 W, Provo, 84604 (801) 357–7056

Gov Agency: Uinta National Forest, 88 West 100 North, Provo, 84601, (801) 342–5100

BIG SPRINGS TRAIL, VIVIAN PARK

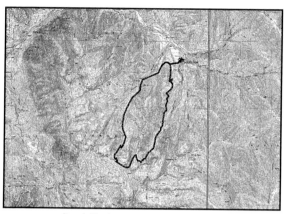

*South Fork canyons are very steep,
however the scenery is beautiful.*

Topo Map: Bridal Veil Falls, # 4011-C5-TF-024
Name of Trailhead: South Fork
Name of Trail: Big Springs Trail, Vivian Park
Trail #: 059
Property of: UNITED STATES FOREST SERVICE
Other Trails used by this route: Shingle Mill Trail - #058
Directions from the closest town to trailhead: Take highway 189 through Provo Canyon to Vivian Park. Follow the Vivian Park Road as it winds southeast. The trailhead is on the southwest side of the highway, just before the Tree Foil Ranch girls scout camp at the end of the road. From highway 189 the trailhead is about 4.5 miles.
Road Conditions: The two lane road is paved the entire route.
Parking instructions: The trailhead is dispersed parking.
    Parking capacity: 15 Trucks and Trailers
Direction of trail from parking area: The trail leaves the trailhead on the west/southwest side, up an old road.

Elevation at T/H: 5900
Highest Elevation: 9850
Steepest Grade: 27%
GPS T/H Longitude: 111°31′ 3.08″N
GPS T/H Latitude: 40°19′ 23.09″W
Number of Feet Climbing: 5000

Camping and use restrictions at trailhead and along route: Weed Free Hay, Camping at Trailhead, Dispersed Camping

Difficulty: Difficult

To complete this route, horses need to be: Very Fit

Trail Route & Directions: Follow the old road up the bench as it winds past the agriculture area. The trail starts about 1/2 mile from the trailhead. The trail splits at that point and either route may be followed. The Big Springs Trail splits west, while the Shingle Mill Trail goes east/southeast.

General description of route: The route starts in open country on an old road. As the route leaves the road, it turns into an alpine area of massive cliffs and rugged terrain. There are several stream crossings along the Big Springs route, and one bridge. Both trails are very steep in places. The Shingle Mill Trail is steep with sharp drop-offs. Portions of this trail see very little use and it is sometimes hard to find. The deep pockets of forest included Bristlecone Pines, Quaken Aspen, steep grassy slopes, Indian Paintbrush, and Blue Penstemon.

Type of Route: Loop

Length of Route in Miles: 12

Estimated travel time: 5.5 Hours

Route Attractions: Scenery, Fishing, Drinking Water, Cell Phone Accessible and Restrooms

Other Attractions: Beautiful scenery, with lots of alpine areas.

Normal Temperatures during recommended months of use:
Spring: Cold to Mild
Summer: Cool to Hot
Fall: Mild to Cold
Months of Accessibility: May to October

Predominant trail surface: Rock, Jeep Trail, Dirt, Loose Rock

Hazards: Bogs, Narrow Bridge, Steep Sections of Trail, Narrow Trail with Steep Drop-offs

Description of Hazards: The one bridge can be used, or can be navigated around.

Current Level of Use:
(High - greater than 7 in group; Low - 3 or less.)
Horsemen: Low
Motorized: None
Bicyclists: Seldom
Hikers: Seldom

Tack & Equipment Dealers: Equus Equestrian Tack & Supply, 6400 N Business Loop Rd, PARK CITY, (435) 615–7433

Police: SUMMIT COUNTY SHERIFF, 6300 Silver Creek Drive, Park City, 84098, (435)615–3500

Veterinarian: Isom Wade P D.V.M., 895 W 100 South, HEBER CITY, 84032, (435) 654–3837

Hospitals: Heber Valley Medical Center, 1485 South Highway 40, HEBER CITY, (435) 654–2500

Gov Agency: Uinta National Forest, 88 West 100 North, Provo, 84601, (801) 342–5100

Other comments: The trailhead is owned by Provo City and is not maintained. Camping is not encouraged.

BLACKHAWK TRAIL, PAYSON CANYON

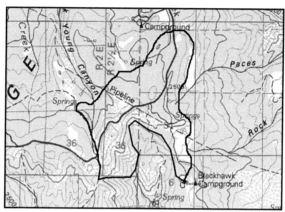

*Payson lakes are north of Blackhawk campground. The trail
is sometimes difficult to find, but worth the effort.*

Topo Map: Payson Lakes, # 39111-H6-TF-024
Name of Trailhead: Blackhawk Campground
Name of Trail: Blackhawk Trail, Payson Canyon
Trail #: 084
Property of: UNITED STATES FOREST SERVICE
Other Trails used by this route: Rock Creek Trail - #101,
Cutoff Trail - #465
Connecting Trails: Loafer Mountain - #908, Blackhawk
Campground Loop - #102, Beaver Dam - #103, Frank
Young Canyon - #097, Holman Canyon - #105, Bear
Trap Ridge - #107, Black Canyon #106, Sawmill
#130.
Directions from the closest town to trailhead: Take I-15 to
Payson. On Highway 6, travel east on East 700 South
Street and follow it about 2 blocks until it turns south
on Canyon Road. Follow Canyon Road up Payson
Canyon approximately 12 miles. Turn east to Black
Hawk Campground, about 2.25 miles.
Road Conditions: The two lane road to Black Hawk is steep

with many sharp turns. The 12 miles to the summit is slow going for a vehicle towing a trailer. The road is closed during the winter months.

Parking instructions: Parking at the equestrian campground is just inside the area at the north end of the large meadow. This is the center of the many equestrian campsites.

Parking capacity: 10 Trucks and Trailers

Direction of trail from parking area: The trail is at the north end of the camping area. From the parking area, follow the road back out of the camping area past the RV dump station. The trail is near the small ridge to the north.

Elevation at T/H: 7900
Highest Elevation: 8460
Steepest Grade: 21%
GPS T/H Longitude: 111°63' 62.80"N
GPS T/H Latitude: 39°90' .35"W
Number of feet Climbing: 2450

Camping and use restrictions at trailhead and along route: Water for Stock, Potable Water, Truck Unloading Ramp, Weed Free Hay, Camping at T/H, Dispersed Camping

Other Restrictions: The equestrian campground is not restricted to horse campers; however, the other campgrounds are not open to horse camping.

Difficulty: Moderate

To complete this route, horses need to be: Moderately Fit

Trail Route & Directions: The trail travels north, northeast crossing the gas pipeline. At about 3 miles the trail turns west and crosses the Nebo Loop highway. The route travels past the Forest Service cabin and the Payson Lakes area. The trail resumes at the end of the dirt road west and south of Payson Lakes, and continues generally south until it again crosses the Nebo Loop highway, about 3 miles from Payson Lakes. Crossing the highway, the route starts east and north loops back to the campground.

General description of route: The route is easy going with steady elevation. It is in an alpine setting with pines, quakes, and open meadows. The trail travels through some steep country on the return to the campground from the east side of the highway. The trail offers beautiful views of the surrounding mountains. The Blackhawk Trail is the center of a network of trails along the Nebo Loop highway.

Type of Route: Loop

Length of Route in Miles: 10

Estimated travel time: 3.5 Hours

Route Attractions: Scenery, Fishing, Conditioning, Drinking Water, RV Facilities, Campsites, Cell Phone Accessible, Restrooms, Provisions for Horses.

Other Attractions: The Nebo area is home to lots of elk and deer. The trailhead is setup for disabled riders, with a loading ramp for wheel chairs. Hitching rails are placed at the equestrian campsites with easy access to potable water.

Normal Temperatures during recommended months of use:
Spring: Cold to Mild
Summer: Mild to Hot
Fall: Mild to Cold
Months of Accessibility: May to November

Predominant trail surface: Rock, Jeep Trail, Dirt

Hazards: Bogs, Steep Sections of Trail, Narrow Trail with Steep Drop-offs, Road Crossings.

Current Level Of Use:
(High - greater than 7 in group; Low - 3 or less.)
Horsemen: Moderate
Motorized: None
Bicyclists: Low
Hikers: Seldom

Tack & Equipment Dealers: Broken Spoke Tack Shop, 898 E 100 North, PAYSON, 84651 - 2347, (801) 465–0904

Police: Utah County Sheriff, 3075 North Main, Spanish Fork, 84660, (801)851–4000

Veterinarian: West Mountain Veterinary Hosp, 143 W 900 North, PAYSON, 84651, (801) 465–4648

Hospitals: Utah Valley Regional MED Center, 1034 N 500 W, Provo, 84604, (801) 357–7056

Gov Agency: Uinta National Forest, 88 West 100 North, Provo, 84601, (801) 342–5100

Other comments: The area southeast of the campground gets steep. Stay on the trails north, west, or south of the campground, or be prepared for bushwhacking in steep areas.

BLUE HILL

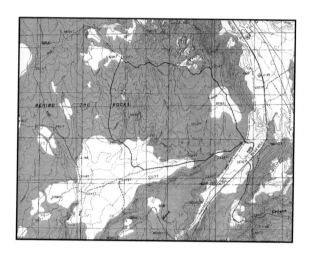

Topo Map: Kane Springs - # 38109-D4-TF-024
Name of Trailhead (T/H): Blue Hill
Name of Trail: Blue Hill
Property of: BLM
Directions from the closest town to trailhead: From Moab
take highway 191 south about 8 miles to the first hill
with a passing lane. Turn right at the top of the hill.
Road Conditions: Paved two lane highway.
Parking instructions: Parking is located immediately after
the cattle-guard.
Parking capacity: 20 Trucks and trailers
Direction of trail from parking area: North

Elevation at T/H: 5520
Highest Elevation: 5720
Steepest Grade: 3%
GPS T/H Longitude: 109°26′ .04″N
GPS T/H Latitude: 038°25′ 5″W
Number of feet Climbing: 565

Camping and use restrictions at trailhead and along route: Weed Free Hay, Camping at Trailhead

Other Restrictions: Clean up after you and your horses. Pick up any manure and dropped hay.

Difficulty: Moderate

To complete this route, horses need to be: Moderately Fit.

Trail Route & Directions: From the parking area, go north along the road to the first well traveled dirt road to the right. Ride north to the red rock domes. Go left and ride down a big sand hill. Stay on the road through a couple of rocky drainages. At the 4-way intersection, ride left, ride south and down to the main road, and east to the parking area. **General description of route:** This route follows jeep track and the main dirt road. This is red rock country with spectacular views.

Type of Route: Loop

Length of Route in Miles: 7

Estimated travel time: 3 Hours

Route Attractions: Scenery, Conditioning, Campsites, Cell Phone Accessible

Normal Temperatures during recommended months of use:

Winter: Chilly to Cold

Spring: Warm to Cool

Summer: Hot

Fall: Warm to cool

Months of Accessibility: Year-round

Predominant trail surface: Sand, Gravel, Rock, Jeep Trail, Dirt, Loose Rock

Hazards: Slick Rock, Steep Sections of Trail, Busy Road Crossings

Description of Hazards: Long weekends bring out the motorized community in large numbers. Watch out for jeeps and ATVs.

Current Level Of Use:
(High - greater than 7 in group; Low - 3 or less.)
Horsemen: Low
Motorized: Moderate
Bicyclists: Moderate
Hikers: Low

Tack & Equipment Dealers: Spanish Valley Feed Store, 2728 S Hwy 191, (435) 259 6315

Police: Moab City Police, Contact: (435) 259–8938 or 911

Veterinarian: Moab Veterinary Clinic, 4575 Spanish Valley Dr, Moab, (435) 259–8710

Hospitals: Allen Memorial Hospital, 719 West Fourth Street, Moab, Tel.1–435–259–7191

Gov Agency: BLM Field Office - Moab, 82 East Dogwood, Moab, 84532, (435) 259–2100

Other comments: The parking area can be very muddy after a big rain storm or snow storm. Flash floods are rare, but can be experienced in this area. Do not ride during a storm.

BLOODY HANDS GAP, WAYNE COUNTY

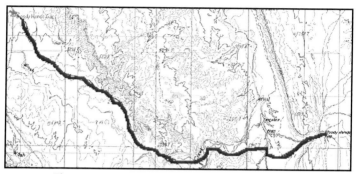

*The pass was marked by native Americans, to indicate
one of the few east-west passages.*

Topo Map: The Post, #37110-G8-TF024
Name of Trail: Bloody Hands Gap, Garfield County
Trail #: Dirt Road
Property of: BUREAU OF LAND MANAGEMENT
Directions from the closest town to trailhead: Turn south
on the Notum Road, which is 20 miles east of Torrey.
Follow the road 7.4 miles to the jeep road leaving east
from Notum Road.
Road Conditions: From Torrey the road is paved to the
Notum Road. Portions of the Notum road is also paved,
but most of it is graded dirt. Travel the dirt road with
caution in wet weather.
Parking instructions: Park along the dirt road or along
the stream area about a quarter mile from the Notum
Road.
Parking capacity: 20 Trucks and Trailers
Direction of trail from parking area: Follow the road
east.

Elevation at T/H: 5280
Highest Elevation: 5280

Steepest Grade: 11%
GPS T/H Longitude: 111°1′ 48.65″N
GPS T/H Latitude: 38°10′ 7.42″W
Number of feet Climbing: 282

Camping and use restrictions at trailhead and along route: Water for Stock, Primitive Camping, Weed Free Hay, Camping at T/H, Dispersed Camping
Difficulty: Easy
To complete this route, horses need to be: Sound Only
Trail Route & Directions: Follow the jeep road east or cut across the open desert.
General description of route: The trail starts out in the river bottoms, in cottonwoods and willows, and on out to the desert country.
Type of Route: Out and Back.
Length of Route in Miles: 8.5
Estimated travel time: 3 Hours
Route Attractions: Scenery, Conditioning, Campsites

Normal Temperatures during recommended months of use:
Winter: Cold to Cool
Spring: Cold to Mild
Fall: Cool to Cold
Months of Accessibility: September to May

Predominant trail surface: Sand, Gravel, Jeep Trail, Loose Rock

Current Level Of Use:
(High - greater than 7 in group; Low - 3 or less.)
Horsemen: Low
Motorized: Low
Bicyclists: Low
Hikers: Low

Tack & Equipment Dealers: JS 2 Tack & Saddlery, 75 E. Main, Wellington, (435) 637–4428

Police: WAYNE COUNTY SHERIFF, Wayne County, Courthouse, Loa, 84747, (435)836–2789

Veterinarian: Animal Hospital, 1989 E. Airport RD., Price, 84501, (435) 637–5797

Hospitals: IHC (Richfield), 1000 N. Main, Venice, 84701, (435) 896–8271

Gov Agency: BUREAU OF LAND MANAGEMENT Field Office - Richfield, 150 East 900 North, Richfield, 84701, (435) 896–1500

Other comments: This is desert country, so take plenty of water for horses and humans.

King Green on his Arab horse looking at the
bloody hand prints that mark the pass.

BOX ELDER, AMERICAN FORK CANYON

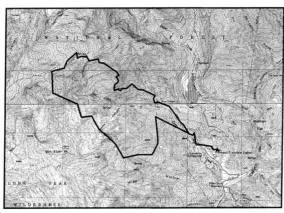

The Box Elder Route features many beautiful vista's, alpine area's and opportunities to view mountain goats. This 13 mile ride takes about 8 hours to travel. It is steep and slow going. The trail has some narrow sections with very steep drop offs.

Topo Map: Timpanogas Cave, # 40111-D5-TF-024
Name of Trailhead: Horse Transfer Station
Name of Trail: Box Elder, American Fork Canyon
Trail #: 044
Property of: UNITED STATES FOREST SERVICE
Other Trails used by this route: White Canyon - #188, Deer Creek - #043
Connecting Trails: Deer Creek Trail - #043
Directions from the closest town to trailhead: From Alpine and Highland, travel east to on highway 92 to American Fork Canyon. Go five miles up the canyon and turn north at the Tibble Fork Reservoir sign. Continue two and half miles to the north end of Tibble Fork Lake and, staying on the paved road, go west 1/2 mile to "Horse Transfer Station" trailhead on the right side of the road.
Road Conditions: Highway 92 is narrow but well main-

tained. Use caution when passing the Timpanogas National Park, where it is 20 miles per hour in the park.

Parking instructions: The parking lot is large; most people parallel park.

Parking capacity: 20 Trucks and trailers

Direction of trail from parking area: Past the trailhead sign on the west side of parking lot.

Elevation at T/H: 6361
Highest Elevation: 9650
Steepest Grade: 22%
GPS T/H Longitude: 111°38' 57.26"N
GPS T/H Latitude: 40°29' 17.86"W
Number of feet Climbing: 3300

Camping and use restrictions at trailhead and along route: Water for Stock, Potable Water, Truck Unloading Ramp, Primitive Camping, Weed Free Hay, Dispersed Camping

Other Restrictions: No camping at trailhead

Difficulty: Very Difficult

To complete this route, horses need to be: Very Fit

Trail Route & Directions: The route heads west out of the parking lot and winds past the west end of the Granite Flat Campground. The trail goes south through a boggy meadow, over a creek, and then up a steep section of the Box Elder trail heading southwest. About 2.5 miles from the trailhead, the White Canyon Trail intersects the Box Elder Trail. Follow the White Canyon Trail northwest to the ridge line 2.5 miles. From the ridge line, continue on the trail going north to the intersection of the White Canyon Trail and the Deer Creek Trail. Follow the Deer Creek Trail east to the trailhead.

General description of route: The route starts out in the pine and aspens and then crosses several steep meadow areas at the higher elevations. The return part of the loop on the Deer Creek Trail starts out crossing a granite area on a narrow trail with a Steep Drop-offs. At one point the same trail crosses a small, slick rock area. After the slick rock area, the trail back is tree covered to the trailhead.

Type of Route: Loop

Length of Route in Miles: 13

Estimated travel time: 5.5 Hours

Route Attractions: Scenery, Drinking Water, Campsites and Provisions for horses.

Other Attractions: Unloading dock for truck loaded horses. Wildlife includes mule, deer, elk, moose, mountain goats, black bear, coyote, badgers, weasels, foxes, and flying squirrels.

Normal Temperatures during recommended months of use:
Spring: Cool to Mild
Summer: Hot
Fall: Mild to Cold
Months of Accessibility: Late May
(snow permitting) to late October

Predominant trail surface: Rock, Jeep Trail, Dirt and Loose Rock

Hazards: Slick Rock, Bogs, Rock Slides, Steep Sections of Trail, Narrow Trail with Steep Drop-offs

Description of Hazards: The White Canyon Trail has some narrow trail sections along some steep drop offs. The trail crews work hard to keep the trail open; however, it can be washed out in some steep areas.

Current Level Of Use:
(High - greater than 7 in group; Low - 3 or less.)
Horsemen: Low
Motorized: None
Bicyclists: None
Hikers: Low

Tack & Equipment Dealers: Highland IFA Country Stores, 521 W 200 North, HIGHLAND, 84003 (801) 756–9604

Police: Utah County Sheriff, 3075 North Main, Spanish Fork, 84660, (801)851–4000

Veterinarian: South Valley Large Animal Clinic, 1791 W 11400 South, SOUTH JORDAN, 84095, (801) 254–2333

Hospitals: Utah Valley Regional MED Center, 1034 N 500 W, Provo, 84604, (801) 357–7056

Gov Agency: Uinta National Forest, 88 West 100 North, Provo, 84601, (801) 342–5100

Other comments: Weather conditions change quickly. Be prepared for sun, wind, snow, rain, and cold and hot weather. This route is not for first time riders or inexperienced horses. Horses should be in great condition, and there are some areas that may need to be hiked. The area was used as a camp for the CCCs during the Great Depression Era. Many of the roads and landscape changes can be attributed to the CCC activities.

*Granite Flats, Deer Creek Trail, near the pass and
connection to the White Canyon Trail.*

BOX ELDER, STANSBURY MOUNTAINS

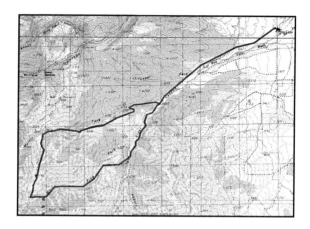

Topo Map: Deseret Peak East - 40112-D5-TF-024
Name of Trailhead (T/H): Box Elder
Name of Trail: Box Elder, Stansbury Mountains
Property of: USFS
Directions from the closest town to trailhead: From main
   street in Grantsville, go south on West Street about 6.3
   miles. There is a sign that looks like a city street sign.
   Make a right (west) and go about a mile to a wide spot
   in the road. This is the best place to park.
Road Conditions: Two lane highway, passable year-round.
Parking instructions: Park along road.
Parking capacity : 5 Trucks and Trailers
Direction of trail from parking area: Southwest along the
   road.

Elevation at T/H: 5430
Highest Elevation: 7770
Steepest Grade: 19%
GPS T/H Longitude: 112°30′ 47.03″W
GPS T/H Latitude: 40°30′ 7.65″N
Number of feet Climbing: 2704

Camping and use restrictions at trailhead and along route: Primitive Camping, Weed Free Hay, Camping at Trailhead, Dispersed Camping

Difficulty: Moderate **To complete this route, horses need to be:** Moderately Fit

Trail Route & Directions: Follow the dirt road west southwest. After about 2.5 miles, the road splits. Keep to the left (southeast) and stay on the dirt road about another mile. You will see a notch in the canyon to the right of the road. There is a dim, two track road that travels through a meadow. Find the old gate in the fence on the other side of the meadow. The trail starts there. It is not a heavily traveled trail. This trail connects with the Stansbury Front Trail. Follow the trail about 3 miles up the canyon. Going over the pass into White Canyon, a water trough can be found. A mile past the trough is a two track, dirt road heading east. Follow the road down the canyon, where it will merge back into the road where it forked on the way out. Follow the road back 2.5 miles to the parking area.

General description of route: This route starts out in the sagebrush flats and climbs up to the quaken aspen and pine trees. The trail is not steep, but is isolated.

Type of Route: Loop

Length of Route in Miles: 15

Estimated travel time: 4 Hours

Route Attractions: Scenery, Conditioning, Drinking Water.

Other Attractions: Plenty of wildlife.

Normal Temperatures during
recommended months of use:
Spring: Cold to Warm
Summer: Cool to Hot
Fall: Warm to Cold
Months of Accessibility: May to November

Predominant trail surface: Jeep Trail, Dirt

Hazards: Steep Sections of Trail.

Description of Hazards: The trail gets very little use and becomes difficult to follow in areas.

Current Level Of Use:
(High - greater than 7 in group; Low - 3 or less.)

Horsemen: Seldom

Motorized: Seldom

Bicyclists: None

Hikers: Seldom

Tack & Equipment Dealers: A. A. Callister Corp, 3615 S Redwood Rd, West Valley City, 84119, (801) 973–7058

Police: TOOELE SHERIFF, 47 S MAIN ST, TOOELE, , (435) 665–2228

Veterinarian: South Valley Large Animal Clinic, 1791 W 11400 South, SOUTH JORDAN, 84095, (801) 254–2333

Hospitals: (Tooele) Mountain West Medical Center, 2055 N Main, TOOELE, (435) 843–3600

Gov Agency: Wasatch-Cache National Forest, 125 South State Street, Salt Lake City, 84138, (801) 236–3400

Other comments: This is a great day ride, with great views of the surrounding mountains and Tooele valley.

COTTONWOOD CANYON

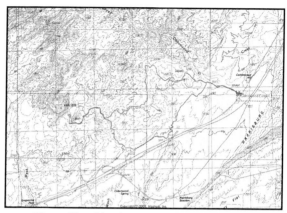

*The trailhead for this entrance to the Red Rock
Tortoise Reserve is a dirt road under I-15.*

Topo Map: Harrisburg Junction, 37113-B4-TF-024
Name of Trailhead (T/H): Cottonwood Canyon
Property of: Local Land
Directions from the closest town to trailhead: On I-15
  northeast of St. George, take the first exit and go southeast about 1.25 miles to the junctions of highways 9
  and 212. Follow the road northeast 1.9 miles towards
  Harrisville. Look for a brown sign between Winkle
  Distributing on the west of the sign and another business on the east. You must use one of these businesses
  driveways to get to the road. Follow the road north
  under I-15 to the trailhead.
Road Conditions: Local, paved two lane roads, and dirt
  accessed by two underpasses under I-15.
Parking instructions: Large circular parking area, park
  along sides.
Parking capacity: 20 Trucks and Trailers
Direction of trail from parking area: The trail can be
  accessed from the northwest corner, over the horse
  friendly gate.

Elevation at T/H: 3390
Highest Elevation: 3617
Steepest Grade: 11%
GPS T/H Longitude: 113°24′ 49″W
GPS T/H Latitude: 037°11′ 3 ″N
Number of feet Climbing: 702

Camping and use restrictions at trailhead and along route: Weed Free Hay, Camping at Trailhead

Other Restrictions: Stay on the trails. No cross country travel is allowed on this portion of the Tortoise preserve. Camping at the trailhead is allowed, but big rigs like motor homes or campers may not fit under I-15.

Difficulty: Easy

To complete this route, horses need to be: Sound Only

Trail Route & Directions: Follow the trail out along the old jeep route. It turns into a trail about a 1/2 mile from the trailhead. The trail travels west through the desert and is slightly uphill. After going over the rise, the trail drops down into a wash just before heading uphill to a pass. From the pass, the trail wraps west south/west and then east, back to the trailhead.

General description of route: This is the Red Rock Tortoise reserve and desert country, with grease wood, sagebrush, and cactus. The trail is sand and red rock. Part of the trail follows the route used by the Escalante party in the 1700s, now know as the Old Spanish Trail.

Type of Route: Loop

Length of Route in Miles: 8 Miles

Estimated travel time: 3 Hours

Route Attractions: Scenery, Campsites, Cell Phone Accessible, Restrooms.

Other Attractions: Trail markings from the Escalante party.

**Normal Temperatures during
recommended months of use:**
Winter: Cool to Cold
Spring: Cool to Cold
Summer: Hot, Hot
Fall: Mild to Cool
Months of Accessibility: September to May

Predominant trail surface: Sand, Gravel, Rock, Jeep
Trail

Current Level Of Use:
(High - greater than 7 in group; Low - 3 or less.)
Horsemen: Low
Motorized: Not Allowed
Bicyclists: Low
Hikers: Low

Tack & Equipment Dealers: Holyoak Saddles, 287 N.
Bluff, St. George, (435) 673–9548
Police: WASHINGTON COUNTY SHERIFF, 750 South
5400 West, Hurricane, 84737, (435)656–6601
Veterinarian: Virgin River Veterinary Clinic, 525 W State
St, Hurricane, (435) 635–4161
Hospitals: River Road IHC Health Center, 577 S. River
Road, St. George, 84790, (435) 688–6100
Gov Agency: Washington County
Other comments: No water can be found most of the year.
Take water for your stock.

DELORES RIVER/COLORADO RIVER AREA

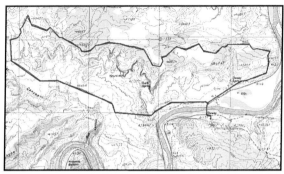

This route follows a dirt jeep road, however cross country travel can be done with very little effort along the south portion of the route.

Map: Dewey - #38109-G3TF-024
Name of Trailhead: Dewey Bridge - Colorado River
Name of Trail: Delores River/Colorado River Area
Property of: BUREAU OF LAND MANAGEMENT
Connecting Trails: By following the road to the east, plenty of the other riding areas can be found along the Delores River.
Directions from the closest town to trailhead: North of Moab is Highway 128, which follows the Colorado River northeast to the Dewey Bridge. At the south end of the bridge, turn east on to the dirt road.
Road Conditions: Highway 128 is a paved, two lane road that winds through the canyon along side the Colorado River.
Parking instructions: Parking is dispersed along jeep trails.
Parking capacity: 50 Trucks and Trailers
Direction of trail from parking area: The trail is north across the bridge and then west/southwest along the road.

Elevation at T/H: 4190
Highest Elevation: 4798
Steepest Grade: 27%
GPS T/H Longitude: 109°18′ 11.37″W
GPS T/H Latitude: 38°48′ 38.36″N
Number of feet Climbing: 1100

Camping and use restrictions at trailhead and along route: Water for Stock, Weed Free Hay, Camping at T/H, Dispersed Camping
Difficulty: Moderate
To complete this route, horses need to be: Sound Only
Trail Route & Directions: Cross the Dewey Bridge going north to the dirt road to the west. Follow the dirt road to the trail/road west. At about 3.5 miles, the road splits; follow the branch on the right (north). The road turns east after about a quarter mile. Follow the road back to the highway and follow the highway south back to the bridge.
General description of route: The route is a jeep trail through the red rock desert. The first three or so miles are fairly flat. As the road turns north, the trail rises up on to the mesa. There is not an established trail or road near the highway, and the last part of the ride is cross-country down some steep slopes.
Type of Route: Loop
Length of Route in Miles: 10
Estimated travel time: 3 Hours
Route Attractions: Scenery, Conditioning, Campsites and Cell Phone Accessible.
Other Attractions: This beautiful red rock country with lots of desert scenery, with plenty of cottonwoods, mesquite and desert flora and fauna.

**Normal Temperatures during
recommended months of use:**
Winter: Cool to Cold
Spring: Cool to Mild
Summer: Hot
Fall: Hot to Cool
Months of Accessibility: September to May

Predominant trail surface: Sand, Gravel, Jeep Trail, Dirt
Hazards: Busy Road Crossings.
Description of Hazards: The route across the Dewey
Bridge rarely has much traffic, but your stock should
be able to remain calm around moving vehicles cross-
ing a bridge.

Current Level Of Use:
(High - greater than 7 in group; Low - 3 or less.)
Horsemen: Low
Motorized: Low
Bicyclists: Seldom
Hikers: Seldom

Tack & Equipment Dealers: Spanish Valley Feed Store,
2728 S Hwy 191, (435) 259 6315
Police: Moab City Police, Contact: (435) 259–8938 or 911
Veterinarian: Moab Veterinary Clinic, 4575 Spanish Valley
Dr, Moab, (435) 259–8710
Hospitals: Allen Memorial Hospital, 719 West Fourth Street,
Moab, Tel.1–435–259–7191
Gov Agency: BUREAU OF LAND MANAGEMENT
Field Office - Moab, 82 East Dogwood, Moab, 84532,
(435) 259–2100

Other comments: This area fills up with four-wheelers and/
or bicycles around the holidays but sees very little traffic on most weekdays. There is very little water in the
area and summers are very hot, so go prepared.

*The Delores River is over the bluff. There is plenty of room
to wander between the Colorado and Delores Rivers.*

DRY CANYON TRAIL, ALPINE

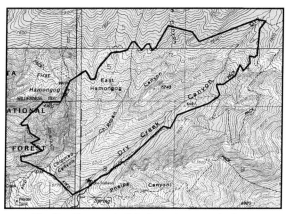

The Dry Canyon trail is the gateway to the Lone Peak Wilderness, from Utah County.

Topo Map: Timpanogos Cave, # 40111-D6-TF-024

Name of Trailhead: Dry Canyon Trailhead

Name of Trail: Dry Canyon Trail, Alpine

Trail #: 043

Property of: UNITED STATES FOREST SERVICE

Connecting Trails: No. Mountain Trail - #042, Deer Creek Trail - #043 , Box Elder Trail - #044

Directions from the closest town to trailhead: Follow highway 74 through Alpine. Turn east on 200 north, travel 2 blocks to 200 east, and turn north. Follow the road (now Grove Drive) past the cemetery and on to the trailhead, about 1600 north.

Road Conditions: The road is paved all of the way to the trailhead. Portions of the two lane road are narrow and winding.

Parking instructions: There is parking along the road, before the trailhead, or dispersed parking at the trailhead. There are two tie rails at the trailhead.

Parking capacity: 15 Trucks and Trailers

Direction of trail from parking area: The trail leaves the trailhead on the northeast.

Elevation at T/H: 5635
Highest Elevation: 7750
Steepest Grade: 24%
GPS T/H Longitude: 111°44′ 55.3″W
GPS T/H Latitude: 40°29′ 2.97″N
Number of feet Climbing: 2540

Camping and use restrictions at trailhead and along route: Weed Free Hay, Camping at T/H, Dispersed Camping

Difficulty: Moderate

To complete this route, horses need to be: Moderately Fit.

Trail Route & Directions: Follow the trail northeast about 1.8 miles to the granite rocks dispersed camping area, just past the water falls to the north of the trail. Follow the trail through the camping area and then north to the creek crossing. The direction of travel changes west/ northwest. Follow the trail to the intersection of the jeep road. Travel down the road to the cut-off trail back to the trailhead.

General description of route: The trail starts up an old jeep road, which continues to the "granite" campground. This portion of the trail is steep and rocky most of the way and crosses the Dry Canyon stream several times. The Mountain Trail is not as steep and is not rocky. It does climb up and down as it passes through several canyons. The return trail/road is steep. The forest includes Douglas fir, limber pine, western spruce, juniper, pinyon and ponderosa pine. Other vegetation includes grasses, mosses, primrose, annuals, and lupine.

Type of Route: Loop
Length of Route in Miles: 5.5
Estimated travel time: 3 Hours
Route Attractions: Scenery, Drinking Water, Campsites, Cell Phone Accessible and Provisions for horses
Other Attractions: The trail is the gateway to many other trails that lead to the Lone Peak Wilderness and American Fork canyon areas. This is diverse habitat that includes mule deer, elk, moose, mountain goats, black bear, coyote, fox, flying squirrels, and many other species.

Normal Temperatures during recommended months of use:
Spring: Cold to Mild
Summer: Warm to Hot
Fall: Warm to Cold
Months of Accessibility: May to October

Predominant trail surface: Rock, Jeep Trail, Dirt
Hazards: Slick Rock, Steep Sections of Trail
Description of Hazards: The Dry Canyon trail is wide, rocky and steep. Some of the stream crossings can be high and swift in the spring. The Mountain Trail is seldom used and sometimes can be hard to find.

Current Level of Use:
(High - greater than 7 in group; Low - 3 or less.)
Horsemen: Low
Motorized: None
Bicyclists: None
Hikers: Low

Tack & Equipment Dealers: Am. Fork IFA Country Stores, 521 W 200 North, AMERICAN FORK, 84003, (801) 756–9604

Police: Utah County Sheriff, 3075 North Main, Spanish Fork, 84660, (801)851–4000

Veterinarian: South Valley Large Animal Clinic, 1791 W 11400 South, SOUTH JORDAN, 84095, (801) 254–2333

Hospitals: Utah Valley Regional MED Center, 1034 N 500 W, Provo, 84604, (801) 357–7056

Gov Agency: Uinta National Forest, 88 West 100 North, Provo, 84601, (801) 342–5100

Other comments: The Dry Canyon area is beautiful any time of year. The scenery is great, as are the vistas.

The trailhead is at the end of Grove Street. There are two tie rails at the trailhead. The trail starts at the boundary of the Lone Peak Wilderness Area.

EAST FORK-BEAR RIVER
TO ALLSOP LAKE

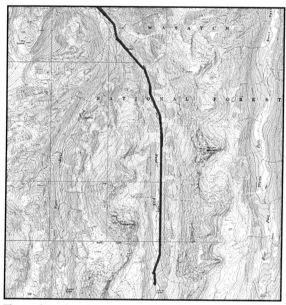

The trail to Alsop lake is a great ride for scenery and fishing.
The trail is easy going for any level of riding ability.

Topo Map: Red Knob, # 40110-G6-TF-024
Name of Trailhead: East Fork-Bear River
Name of Trail: East Fork-Bear River to Allsop Lake
Trail #: 100
Property of: UNITED STATES FOREST SERVICE
Other Trails used by this route: Left Hand Fork–#151
Connecting Trails: Right Hand Fork - #100, Bear River,
  Smiths Fork Trail - #091

Directions from the closest town to trailhead: On highway 150 south of Evanston, Wyoming, travel to the
  Utah border. From the border, travel about 6 miles
  to the road turning east. (The road is about a quarter
  mile north of the East Fork Campground.) Follow the

road about 1.25 miles as it curves northeast. The road turns east again about a quarter mile. Turn on the dirt road going south. Follow the dirt road south/southeast about five miles to the trailhead.

Road Conditions: Highway 150 is well maintained, but closed during the winter. The dirt logging road is graded and well maintained. It is a fairly wide road but, wash boardy.

Parking instructions: Parking is made more for cars without trailers. Park anywhere; the parking lot is rarely full.

Parking capacity : 10 Trucks and Trailers

Direction of trail from parking area: The trail is east of the parking lot and outhouse.

Elevation at T/H: 9018
Highest Elevation: 10574
Steepest Grade: 10%
GPS T/H Longitude: 110°45′ 21.96″W
GPS T/H Latitude: 40°51′ 39.33″N
Number of feet Climbing: 933

Camping and use restrictions at trailhead and along route: Water For Stock, Primitive Camping, Weed Free Hay, Camping at T/H, Dispersed Camping

Other Restrictions: Allsop Lake is in the High Uinta's Wilderness area. Wilderness restrictions apply.

Difficulty: Moderate

To complete this route, horses need to be: Sound Only

Trail Route & Directions: Trail #100 goes southeast about 3.5 miles and forks south. Follow the left (eastern) trail #151 and continue southeast about another 5 miles to the lake.

General description of route: The route is easy going and only climbs 1,000 feet in ten miles. The trail is covered by a forest of pines and Quaken Aspen, running up a glacial cirque and crossing several streams along the way. The canyon walls are steep to cliff like, with no trails leading out of the canyon as it approaches the lake area. Allsop Lake is a beautiful lake situated in a small basin at the head of the East Fork Drainage.

Type of Route: Out and Back.

Length of Route in Miles: 17

Estimated travel time: 5 Hours

Route Attractions: Scenery, Fishing, Conditioning, Drinking Water, Campsites and Restrooms.

Other Attractions: Allsop Lake is one of the few lakes in the area that has native cutthroat trout that are sustained by natural reproduction. The area is also home to numerous moose, elk, and deer.

Normal Temperatures during recommended months of use:
Spring: Cold to Cool
Summer: Cool to Warm
Fall: Warm to Cold
Months of Accessibility: June to October

Predominant trail surface: Dirt, Loose Rock

Hazards: Slick Rock, Bogs, Narrow Trail with Steep Drop-offs

Description of Hazards: There is a short part of the trail that is narrow with a steep drop-off.

Current Level of Use:
(High - greater than 7 in group; Low - 3 or less.)
Horsemen: Low
Motorized: Not Allowed
Bicyclists: Not Allowed
Hikers: Low

Tack & Equipment Dealers: Lazy Sb Leather & Saddlery, FT BRIDGER, WY 82933, (307) 782–7300

Police: MOUNTAIN VIEW SHERIFF, 77 COUNTY ROAD 109, EVANSTON, WY, (307) 782–3682

Veterinarian: Bear River Veterinary Clinic, 619 Almy Road #107, N OF EVANSTON, WY, (307) 789–5230

Hospitals: Evanston Regional Hospital, 190 Arrowhead Dr., Evanston, WY 82930 - 9266, (307) 789–3636

Gov Agency: Wasatch-Cache National Forest, 125 South State Street, Salt Lake City, 84138, (801) 236–3400

Other comments: It is a great one night camping area, with grassy meadows for feed and spring water. Allsop Lake is a great fishery; take a fishing pole! Horse feed for overnight camping may be scarce during the later part of the year. This area is grazed by livestock. Check with the Forest Service for feed conditions.

FIFTHS WATER, LOWER & UPPER TRAILS

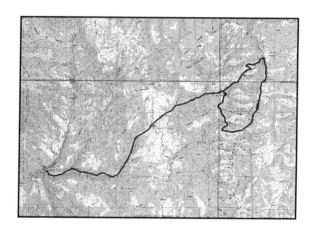

Topo Map: Rays Valley, #40111-A3-TF-024 & Strawberry NW

Name of Trailhead (T/H): Three Forks Trailhead

Name of Trail: Fifths Water, Lower & Upper Trails

Trail #: 015

Property of: United States Forest Service

Connecting Trails: Center Trail - #009, Cottonwood Second Water - #018.

Directions from the closest town to trailhead: From Spanish Fork Canyon, US Highway 6, turn north at the Diamond Fork road #029, about 6 miles from the mouth of Spanish Fork Canyon. Travel northeast up Diamond Fork about 10 miles to Three Forks Trailhead.

Road Conditions: Both highways are open year round. Highway 6 is very busy, so use caution.

Parking capacity: 6 Trucks and Trailers

Direction of trail from parking area: The trail leaves the parking lot from the east.

Elevation at T/H: 5680
Highest Elevation: 8300
Steepest Grade: 12%
GPS T/H Longitude: 111°21' 16.07"W
GPS T/H Latitude: 40°05' 3.84"N
Number of feet Climbing: 3130

Camping and use restrictions at trailhead and along route: Water For Stock, Weed Free Hay, Camping at Trailhead, Dispersed Camping

Difficulty: Moderate

To complete this route, horses need to be: Moderately Fit

Trail Route & Directions: Follow the trail east from the parking lot. The going is uphill along the Fifth Water Creek to the Sheep Creek Trailhead. The "Upper Trail" leaves the trailhead northeast from the trail-head. Follow it to the Strawberry Ridge or the Deep Vat Road.

Type of Route: Out and Back.

Length of Route in Miles: 8

Estimated travel time: 3 Hours

Route Attractions: Scenery, Campsites and Cell Phone Accessible.

Other Attractions: While this route is out and back, many connecting trails make loop back routes possible.

Normal Temperatures during
recommended months of use:
Summer: Cool to Hot
Fall: Cool to Mild
Months of Accessibility: May to October

Predominant trail surface: Rock, Jeep Trail, Dirt, Loose Rock

Current Level of Use:
(High - greater than 7 in group; Low - 3 or less.)
Horsemen: Low
Motorized: Moderate
Bicyclists: Seldom
Hikers: Seldom

Tack & Equipment Dealers: Broken Spoke Tack Shop, 898 E 100 North, PAYSON, 84651 - 2347, (801) 465–0904.

Police: UTAH COUNTY SHERIFF, Provo, 84603, (801)343–4001

Veterinarian: West Mountain Veterinary Hosp, 143 W 900 North, PAYSON, 84651, (801) 465–4648

Hospitals: Springville IHC Health Center, 385 S. 400 E., Springville, 84663, (801) 489–3244

Gov Agency: Uinta National Forest, 88 West 100 North, Provo, 84601, (801) 342–5100

HAMONGOG TRAIL

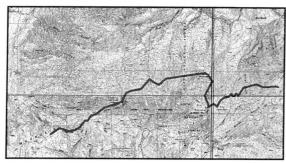

The Hamongog trail travels through some rough, steep mountains. The views of Utah County and Timpanogas are very impressive.

Topo Map: Lehi, #40111-D7-TF-024, Draper, 40111-E7-TF-024, Dromedary Peak, 40111-E6-TF-024, Timpanogas Cave 40111-D6-TF-024

Name of Trailhead: Corner Canyon Road

Name of Trail: Hamongog Trail

Trail #: 187

Property of: UNITED STATES FOREST SERVICE

Other Trails used by this route: North Mountain Trail, #042

Connecting Trails: Dry Canyon, #043, Lake Hardy, #176, Lone Peak, #186.

Directions from the closest town to trailhead: In Draper, go to 1300 East and 123000 South. Turn south and follow the roundabout east to Pioneer Road. From Pioneer Road, turn south on 2000 East and follow it to the dirt road. Follow the dirt road about 2.8 miles to the parking area. The parking area is an overlook just south of the dirt road.

Road Conditions: The road is a paved two lane highway through Draper to the dirt road going to Corner Canyon. The dirt road is graded and well maintained, but can be quite treacherous when wet, especially when pulling a stock trailer.

Parking instructions: Park at the overlook.

Parking capacity: 10 Trucks and Trailers

Direction of trail from parking area: The trail is northeast of the parking lot across the dirt road.

Elevation at T/H: 5870
Highest Elevation: 8290
Steepest Grade: 35%
GPS T/H Longitude: 111°49′ 0.89″W
GPS T/H Latitude: 40°29′ 39.35″N
Number of feet Climbing: 1,927

Camping and use restrictions at trailhead and along route: Water for Stock, Dispersed Camping

Difficulty: Difficult

To complete this route, horses need to be: Very Fit

Trail Route & Directions: The route follows an old jeep trail the first part of the journey along a ridge. As the jeep trail ends about 1.5 miles from the trail head, the trail picks up going north for short distance, then continues northeast until it reaches a bowl called the Second Hemongog. At that point the trail turns south until it reaches the North Mountain Trail. The North Mountain Trail continues on until it intersects with the Dry Canyon Trail.

General description of route: The trail starts in the scrub oaks on a jeep track and stays in them until the trail starts. From there, the trail gets very steep, with some areas of Steep Drop-offs along a narrow trail. This trail does not get a lot of use and can be difficult to find, especially the farther you get from the trailhead.

Type of Route: Out and Back

Length of Route in Miles: 14

Estimated travel time: 5 Hours

Route Attractions: Scenery and Drinking Water.

Other Attractions: There are a few small streams along the way to water the stock. The area is home to mule deer, elk, and black bears.

Normal Temperatures during recommended months of use:
Spring: Cold to Mild
Summer: Hot
Fall: Cool to Cold
Months of Accessibility: May to October

Predominant trail surface: Rock, Jeep Trail, Dirt, Loose Rock

Hazards: Steep Sections of Trail, Narrow Trail with Steep Drop-offs

Description of Hazards : The trail is narrow in places.

Current Level Of Use:
(High - greater than 7 in group; Low - 3 or less.)
Horsemen: Low
Motorized: None
Bicyclists: None
Hikers: Low

Tack & Equipment Dealers: Draper IFA Country Stores, 1071 E Pioneer Rd., Draper, 84020, (801) 571–0125

Police: Salt Lake County Sheriff, 2001 S State, Salt Lake City, 84190, (801) 468–3931

Veterinarian: South Valley Large Animal Clinic, 1791 W 11400 South, SOUTH JORDAN, 84095, (801) 254–2333

Hospitals: Alta View Hospital, 9660 S 1300 E, Sandy, 84094, 801) 501–2600

Gov Agency: Uinta National Forest, 88 West 100 North,

Provo, 84601, (801) 342–5100

Other comments: This route can be a loop trail by continuing down the Dry Canyon Trail and then working back to the Hemongog Trail.

The trailhead is an overlook on the southwest side of the dirt road. The trail is on the opposite side of the road.

HIGHLINE TRAIL, HIGH UINTAS WILDERNESS

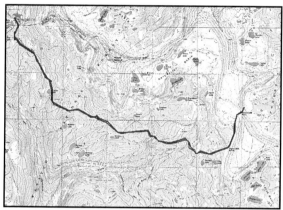

The Highline Trail winds from the Mirror Lake area to the west, all the way to the Flaming Gorge area, about 125 miles.

Topo Map: Hayden Peak, # 40110-F7-TF-024
Name of Trailhead: Highline Trailhead to Rocky Sea Pass
Name of Trail: Highline Trail, High Uintas Wilderness
Trail #: 083 and 025
Property of: UNITED STATES FOREST SERVICE
Connecting Trails: Mirror Lake Trail, Packard
 Lake - #059, Naturalist Basin - #084, Lake Trail -
 #089, Four Lakes Basin - #102
Directions from the closest town to trailhead: Traveling
 east from Kamas on highway 150, go 36 miles. The
 trailhead is about 3 miles past Mirror Lake. There are
 two trailheads; the trailhead to the north is the equestrian trailhead.
Road Conditions: Highway 150 is well maintained but
 closed during the winter months.
Parking instructions: The parking lot is large. Parking is
 not marked, and parking is allowed anywhere in the
 area.

Parking capacity: 15 Trucks and Trailers
Direction of trail from parking area: The trail is southeast
   of the parking lot, past the hikers parking lot.

Elevation at T/H: 10300
Highest Elevation: 11277
Steepest Grade: 13%
GPS T/H Longitude: 110°51′ 51.10″W
GPS T/H Latitude: 040°43′ 22.4″N
Number of feet Climbing: 1830

Camping and use restrictions at trailhead and along route:
   Water For Stock, Potable Water, Truck Unloading
   Ramp, Primitive Camping, Weed Free Hay, Camping
   at T/H, Dispersed Camping
Other Restrictions: Groups are restricted to 13 horses and
   12 riders.
Difficulty: Moderate
To complete this route, horses need to be: Moderately
   Fit.
Trail Route & Directions: Follow the trail southeast from
   the trailhead past the hikers trailhead. Then follow it
   south/southeast past the Pinto Lake trail. As the trail
   passes the Pinto Lake trail, it climbs east/northeast
   past Pigeon Milk Springs and then North to Rocky Sea
   Pass.
General description of route: The trail starts out in a pine
   and quakes forest and continues in the forest to Pigeon
   Milk Springs. There are many streams, bogs, and creek
   crossings. The trail is wide and very rocky most of the
   way.
Type of Route: Out and Back
Length of Route in Miles: 15
Estimated travel time: 6 Hours
Route Attractions: Scenery, Fishing, Conditioning,

Drinking Water, Campsites, Restrooms, Provisions for horses.

Other Attractions: This route is in part of the High Uinta's Wilderness Area, with trails leading to Naturalist Basin, Granddaddy's Lake region, Four Lakes Basin, and many other wilderness areas.

Normal Temperatures during recommended months of use:
Spring: Cold to Warm
Summer: Cool to Hot
Fall: Cool to Cold
Months of Accessibility: June to October

Predominant trail surface: Gravel, Rock, Dirt, Loose Rock

Other surfaces: Many of the boggy areas are covered with wood bridges.

Hazards: Deep or Wide Water Crossings, Bogs, Narrow Bridges, Narrow Trail with Steep Drop-offs.

Description of Hazards: This is a wilderness area. The weather conditions can change rapidly. The Uintas is a vast area that requires preparation and a knowledge of the backcountry. Getting turned around and lost is a real possibility.

Current Level of Use:
(High - greater than 7 in group; Low - 3 or less.)
Horsemen: Moderate
Motorized: Not Allowed
Bicyclists: Not Allowed
Hikers: Moderate

Tack & Equipment Dealers: Equus Equestrian Tack & Supply, 6400 N Business Loop Rd, PARK CITY, (435) 615–7433

Police: SUMMIT COUNTY SHERIFF, 6300 Silver Creek Drive, Park City, 84098, (435)615–3500

Veterinarian: Arcadia Veterinary Clinic, 90 E 1520 N Hwy 40, Heber, (435) 654–0592

Hospitals: Heber Valley Medical Center, 1485 South Highway 40, HEBER CITY, , (435) 654–2500

Gov Agency: Wasatch-Cache National Forest, 125 South State Street, Salt Lake City, 84138, (801) 236–3400

Other comments: Go prepared for any type of weather, loss of horse shoes, etc.

Rocky Sea Pass is 7.5 miles from the Highline Trailhead highway 150, near Mirror Lake. This photo is of the trail on the west side of Rocky Sea Pass.

One of many meadows along the Highline Trail.

HOLBROOK CANYON, DAVIS COUNTY

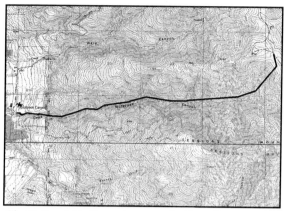

The Holbrook Trail travels east to the Great Western Trail.

Topo Map: Bountiful Peak, USGF # 40111-H7-TF-024
Name of Trailhead: Holbrook Canyon
Name of Trail: Holbrook Canyon, Davis County
Property of: UNITED STATES FOREST SERVICE
Connecting Trails: Great Western Trail
Directions from the closest town to trailhead: The trailhead is in Bountiful on the high bench near the LDS Temple. From I-15, follow 400 North east to 1300 East. Turn south on 1300 East. The trailhead is about a mile. Look for it on the east side of the road, just south of the LDS Temple.
Road Conditions: All of the roads are locally maintained and asphalt.
Parking instructions: The parking lot is small. Parking on the street is allowed.
Parking capacity: 7 Trucks and Trailers
Direction of trail from parking area: The trail is east of the parking area.

Elevation at T/H: 4,860
Highest Elevation: 8,400
Steepest Grade: 20%
GPS T/H Longitude: 111°51′ 10.66″W
GPS T/H Latitude: 040°52′ 52.96″N
Number of feet Climbing: 4,182

Camping and use restrictions at trailhead and along route: Water for Stock, Weed Free Hay, Dispersed Camping
Difficulty: Moderate
To complete this route, horses need to be: Moderately Fit
Trail Route & Directions: This route generally travels east along the Holbrook Creek, ending at the Great Western Trail.
General description of route: The trail is covered by Maple and Gambels Oak and follows a fast moving creek. It is a short route that climbs 4,000 feet in four miles.
Type of Route: Out and Back.
Length of Route in Miles: 8
Estimated travel time: 3.5 Hours
Route Attractions: Scenery, Drinking Water, Campsites, Cell Phone Accessible.

Normal Temperatures during recommended months of use:
Spring: Cold to Warm
Summer: Warm to Hot
Fall: Cool to Cold
Months of Accessibility: May to October

Predominant trail surface: Rock, Jeep Trail, Dirt, Loose Rock
Hazards: Bogs, Steep Sections of Trail

Current Level of Use:
(High - greater than 7 in group; Low - 3 or less.)
Horsemen: Low
Motorized: None
Bicyclists: Seldom
Hikers: Moderate

Tack & Equipment Dealers: A. A. Callister Corp, 3615 S Redwood Rd., West Valley City, 84119, (801) 973–7058

Police: DAVIS COUNTY SHERIFF, 800 West State St., Farmington, 84025, (801) 451–4120

Veterinarian: Animal Medical Clinic, 463 W. 500 S., Bountiful, (801) 292–8228

Hospitals: South Davis Community Hospital, 401 S 400 E, Bountiful, 84010, (801) 295–2361

Gov Agency: Wasatch-Cache National Forest, 125 South State Street, Salt Lake City, 84138, (801) 236–3400

Other Comments: Over a period of six or more years, the Holbrook Canyon trail was carved out by a local member of Backcountry Horsemen of Utah. King Green started the work on the trail after he retired. By taking the Great Western trail and some other connecting trails, it is possible to travel from Bountiful to Morgan, Utah.

HORSESHOE CANYON, CANYON LANDS NATIONAL PARK

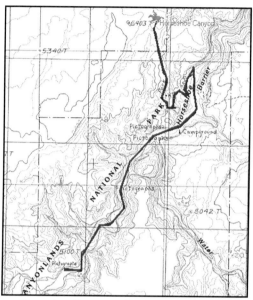

Horseshoe Canyon is detached from the main portion Canyonlands National Park.

Topo Map: Sugar Loaf Butte, #38110-D2-TF-024

Name of Trailhead: Horseshoe Canyon

Name of Trail: Horseshoe Canyon, Canyon Lands National Park

Property of: Canyon Lands National Park

Connecting Trails: There are two trails leaving the canyon on the east side. The trail in the bottom of the canyon continues out of the park, to the south, into the Robbers Roost area.

Directions from the closest town to trailhead: 19 miles northeast of Hanksville, or 24.5 miles southwest of I-70 on highway 24 (across the highway from Goblin Valley turn-off), turn southeast on the dirt road marked for Hans Flat and Canyonlands. Follow the dirt road 24 miles to the fork in the road. Follow the northeast (left) fork. There is an instructional kiosk at the fork in the road. From the fork, follow the road 5.25 miles to the dirt road the turns southeast to the trailhead. It is about 1.75 miles to the trailhead.

Road Conditions: Highway 24 is a paved two lane highway. The dirt roads to the trailhead are well maintained, graded roads. The last dirt road to the trailhead is a little rough, but passable with a truck and trailer.

Parking instructions: The parking area is a large, dispersed parking area.

Parking capacity: 20 Trucks and Trailers

Direction of trail from parking area: The trail is in the southeast corner of the parking lot near the information kiosk.

Elevation at T/H: 5,247
Highest Elevation: 5,247
Steepest Grade: 29%
GPS T/H Longitude: 110°11′ 59.11″W
GPS T/H Latitude: 38°28′ 25.67″N
Number of feet Climbing: 767

Camping and use restrictions at trailhead and along route: Weed Free Hay, Camping at T/H, Dispersed Camping

Other Restrictions: The trail is blocked by a gate that is locked. To get the combination for the lock, call (435)259–4351. The Hans Flat ranger's office will give you the combination and a permit to use the trail. There are restrictions as to the number of horses and where the horses can travel. Check with the ranger's office for the restrictions.

Difficulty: Moderate

To complete this route, horses need to be: Moderately Fit.

Trail Route & Directions: Follow the trail past the kiosk and the first gate. The trail winds down the slick rock to the bottom of the canyon and turns south, up the canyon.

General description of route: This spectacular route varies from slick rock to sand, from desert to oasis, and from steep to flat. The route starts down the Navajo Sandstone cliffs and ends up in the canyon, which it overlooks. There is usually water in the canyon to water the horses. Horseshoe Canyon is covered with cottonwoods, willows, and marshes, with some tamarisde and blackbrush.

Type of Route: Out and Back.

Length of Route in Miles: 7

Estimated travel time: 4 Hours

Route Attractions: Scenery, Conditioning, Drinking Water and Restrooms.

Other Attractions: The Grand Gallery is a world famous pictograph and is part of many pictographs in the area. It is one of the largest ever discovered. Wildlife includes mule deer, red foxes, hawks, bobcats, and antelope.

Normal Temperatures during recommended months of use:

Spring: Cold to Cool

Summer: Hot

Fall: Mild to Cold

Months of Accessibility: April to September

Predominant trail surface: Sand, Gravel, Rock, Jeep Trail, Dirt, Loose Rock

Hazards: Slick Rock, Steep Sections of Trail, Narrow Trail with Steep Drop-offs

Description of Hazards: The trail leading in and out of the canyon is an old road but is steep, rocky and has a section of slickrock.

Current Level of Use:
(High - greater than 7 in group; Low - 3 or less.)
Horsemen: Low
Motorized: None
Bicyclists: None
Hikers: Moderate

Tack & Equipment Dealers: Burns Saddlery Inc., 79 W. Main, Salina, 84654, (434) 529–7484

Police: WAYNE COUNTY SHERIFF, Wayne County Courthouse, Loa, 84747, (435) 836–2789

Veterinarian: Animal Hospital, 1989 E. Airport Rd., Price, 84501, (435) 637–5797

Hospitals: Green River Medical Center, 305 W. Main, Green River, . (435) 564–3434

Gov Agency: Canyon Lands National Park, 2282 SW Resource Blvd, Moab, 84532, (435)719–2313

Other comments: The area is desert and the conditions can be extreme. Take plenty of water and expect sudden changes in the weather.

*Horses are welcomed to Horseshoe Canyon, but by (free)
permit only. The trail leading into the canyon is
an old road, carved out of a cliff.*

HOLT DRAW, WEST OF TORREY

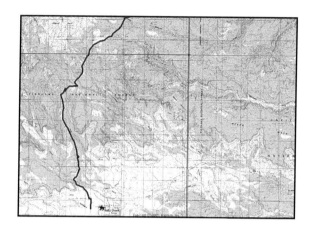

Topo Map: Torrey, 38111-C4-TF-024
Name of Trailhead (T/H): The City of Torrey
Name of Trail: Holt Draw, West of Torrey
Trail #: 146
Property of: USFS
Other Trails used by this route: Great Western Trail - #147
Directions from the closest town to trailhead: Travel east from Torrey 1/4 mile and turn north on the dirt road. Park at the trailhead about 1/8th mile north of the highway.
Road Conditions: From Torrey, the highway is a two lane and paved.
Parking instructions: Park at the trailhead or anywhere in the area along the road.
Parking capacity: 50 Trucks and Trailers
Direction of trail from parking area: Follow the jeep road about four miles to the trail. The trail leaves the road on the northeast side of the road.

Elevation at T/H: 6,940
Highest Elevation: 8,398
Steepest Grade: 10%
GPS T/H Longitude: 111°25′ 53.54″W
GPS T/H Latitude: 038°18′ 3.40″N
Number of feet Climbing: 1,659

Camping and use restrictions at trailhead and along route: Weed Free Hay, Camping at Trailhead, Dispersed Camping

Difficulty: Moderate

To complete this route, horses need to be: Moderately Fit

Trail Route & Directions: Follow the jeep track north about four miles to the trail. Keep to the right as the road passes two roads on the left (west). The trail travels northeast from Holt canyon and ends at Paradise Flats.

General description of route: The route starts out in the desert highlands and travels to the alpine areas of Fishlake National Forest. The desert floor is vegetated by rabbitbrush, sagebrush, mesquite, and junipers. The national forest is populated with Quaken Aspen, Ponderosa, and Pinyon pines. The route rises slowly through the desert and gets continually steeper as it winds through the national forest.

Type of Route: Out and Back.

Length of Route in Miles: 20

Estimated travel time: 5 Hours

Route Attractions: Scenery, Conditioning, Cell Phone Accessible.

Other Attractions: The view from Paradise Flats is of the red rock areas around Torrey. It overlooksCapital Reef National Park and the Waterpocket Fold in the distance.

Normal Temperatures during recommended months of use:
Spring: Cold to Cool
Summer: Mild to Warm
Fall: Mild to Cold
Months of Accessibility: March to October

Predominant trail surface: Jeep Trail, Dirt, Loose Rock
Hazards: Steep Sections of Trail.
Description of Hazards: There are several steep sections of the trail after leaving the jeep trail.

Current Level of Use:
(High - greater than 7 in group; Low - 3 or less.)
Horsemen: Low
Motorized: Seldom
Bicyclists: Seldom
Hikers: Seldom

Tack & Equipment Dealers: Burns Saddlery Inc., 79 W. Main, Salina, 84654, (434) 529–7484
Police: WAYNE COUNTY SHERIFF, Wayne County Courthouse, Loa, 84747, (435)836–2789
Veterinarian: Tri County Veterinary Hospital, 325 E. 200 N., Torrey, (435) 836–3487
Hospitals: Sevier Valley Hospital IHC, 1100 N. Main, Richfield, (435) 896–8271
Gov Agency: Dixie National Forest, 1789 Wedgewood Lane, Cedar City, 84720, (435) 865–3700
Other comments: There is very little water for stock in the area, and some water at Paradise Flats.

JORDAN RIVER PARKWAY TO WILLOWS CAMPGROUND

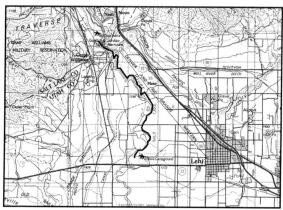

The Jordan River Parkway from the old Bluffdale Arena, travels from just north of Camp Williams and on to Utah Lake. This map shows the route to the Willows Campground.

Topo Map: Jordan Narrows 40111-D8-TF-024

Name of Trailhead: Jordan Narrows

Name of Trail: Jordan River Parkway to Willows Campground

Property of: Bluffdale City

Directions from the closest town to trailhead: On Redwood Road, from Bluffdale or Lehi, go to 17000 So. (Jordan Narrows Road) and turn east. Follow the road as it turns north to the old Bluffdale Arena. Park in the arena parking lot.

Road Conditions: The road is paved to the parking lot.

Parking instructions: Park anywhere in the lot.

Parking capacity: 20 Trucks and Trailers

Direction of trail from parking area: The trail is somewhat difficult to find. Travel southeast from the parking lot. The trail crosses the road about 1/4 mile from the trailhead.

Elevation at T/H: 4,625
Highest Elevation: 4,625
Steepest Grade: 21%
GPS T/H Longitude: 111°55′ 37.51″W
GPS T/H Latitude: 40°26′ 43.91″N
Number of feet Climbing: 934

Camping and use restrictions at trailhead and along route: Water for Stock

Other Restrictions: Much of the route is asphalt with a dirt path beside it in some areas. Some travel on the asphalt is necessary.

Difficulty: Easy

To complete this route, horses need to be: Sound Only

Trail Route & Directions: The route generally meanders south along the Jordan River.

General description of route: The trail has very few trees or brush. Near the Bluffdale Arena, there is a wide bridge that crosses the Jordan River. On the east side of the trail, the route passes the beautiful Thanksgiving Point golf course. Most of the remaining route passes private property on either side.

Type of Route: Out and Back.

Length of Route in Miles: 11.6

Estimated travel time: 3 Hours

Route Attractions: Fishing, Conditioning, Cell Phone Accessible and Restrooms.

Other Attractions: The Willows Campground and picnic area does have some picnic tables. It's a great place to stop for lunch.

**Normal Temperatures during
recommended months of use:**
Winter: Cool To
Cold **Spring:** Cool to Mild
Summer: Hot
Fall: Cool to Cold
Months of Accessibility: Year round

Predominant trail surface: Dirt.
Other surfaces: There is an asphalt path for other trail users.
Description of Hazards: A wide bridge crosses the river just north of Thanksgiving Point golf course.

Current Level of Use:
(High - greater than 7 in group; Low - 3 or less.)
Horsemen: Low
Motorized: None
Bicyclists: Moderate
Hikers: Moderate

Tack & Equipment Dealers: Draper IFA Country Stores, 1071 E Pioneer Rd, Draper, 84020, (801) 571–0125
Police: Salt Lake County Sheriff, 2001 S State, Salt Lake City, 84190, (801) 468–3931
Veterinarian: South Valley Large Animal Clinic, 1791 W 11400 South, SOUTH JORDAN, 84095, (801) 254–2333
Hospitals: Alta View Hospital, 9660 S 1300 E, Sandy, 84094, (801) 501–2600
Gov Agency: Bluffdale City, 14175 South Redwood Road, Bluffdale, 84065, (801) 254–2200
Other comments: The trail continues on south to Utah Lake.

This bridge crosses the Jordan River near Thanksgiving Point.

Timpanogas Mountain as seen from Jordan River Parkway.

LITTLE GRAND CANYON, BUCK HORN WASH

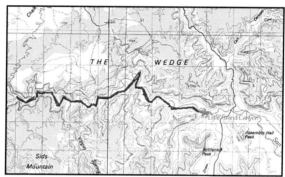

*Little Grand Canyon is easy to follow along the San Rafael River,
the scenery includes sand stone cliffs with some
arches and beautiful river bottoms.*

Topo Map: Bottle Neck Peak, #39110-A6-TF-024
Name of Trailhead: San Rafael Bridge Campground
Name of Trail: Little Grand Canyon, Buck Horn Wash
Property of: BUREAU OF LAND MANAGEMENT
Directions from the closest town to trailhead: From the center of Huntington, traveling south on highway 10, go about 7.5 miles to the dirt road traveling east. It is about 1.6 miles north from the center of Castle Dale. Follow the dirt road 25 miles to the San Rafael Bridge Campground. The campground is on the east side of the road after crossing the bridge. Just past the campground as the road bends, there is a dirt road. Follow that road west about a 1/4 mile to the trailhead area.
Road Conditions: The highway is paved and maintained to the dirt road leaving highway 10. It is dirt all the way to the campground and trailhead. Although the area is dry most of the year, the dirt roads can be impassable when wet.
Parking instructions: This is a dispersed parking area. It is

a large area that could accommodate 50 rigs or more.

Parking capacity : 50 Trucks and Trailers

Direction of trail from parking area: The trail can be found north of the trailhead along the San Rafael River.

Elevation at T/H: 5,130
Highest Elevation: 5627
Steepest Grade: 26%
GPS T/H Longitude: 110°41' 6.48"W
GPS T/H Latitude: 39°4' 38.72"N
Number of feet Climbing: 380

Camping and use restrictions at trailhead and along route: Water for Stock, Weed Free Hay, Camping at T/H, Dispersed Camping

Other Restrictions: The canyon is fenced off for cattle grazing. Leave gates as you find them, either closed or open.

Difficulty: Easy

To complete this route, horses need to be: Sound Only.

Trail Route & Directions: The trail is well traveled and easy to follow along the San Rafael River. The beginning part of the trail is an old jeep road that ends near the first gate.

General description of route: The Little Grand Canyon is beautiful year round, with high sandstone cliffs and shale. The San Rafael River winds lazily at the foot of the cliffs and through the river bottoms. There are some narrow parts of the trail with some Steep Drop-offs. The area has many geological changes, from Tununk and Mancos Shale to Navajo Sandstone.

Type of Route: Out and Back

Length of Route in Miles: 20

Estimated travel time: 7 Hours

Route Attractions: Scenery, Fishing, Conditioning,

Drinking Water, Campsites and Restrooms.

Other Attractions: There are restrooms and RV facilities at the San Rafael Bridge Campground. Across the dirt road from the campground is an old, run down corral that may or may not be suitable to hold livestock.

Normal Temperatures during recommended months of use:
Winter: Cold
Spring: Cold To Mild
Summer: Hot
Fall: Mild to Cold

Months of Accessibility: Travel can be year round; however, summer can be very hot and dry. Winter can be snowy.

Predominant trail surface: Sand, Gravel, Jeep Trail

Other surfaces: The trail travels across the river in some areas.

Hazards: Slick Rock, Deep or Wide Water Crossings, Steep Sections of Trail and Narrow Trail with Steep Drop-offs.

Description of Hazards: The narrow portion of the trail—with steep drop-offs—is short, as are the few other steep sections.

Current Level of Use:
(High - greater than 7 in group; Low - 3 or less.)
Horsemen: Low
Motorized: None
Bicyclists: Seldom
Hikers: Moderate

Tack & Equipment Dealers: Burns Saddlery Inc., 79 W. Main, Salina, 84654, (434) 529–7484

Police: EMERY COUNTY SHERIFF, P.O. Box 514, Castle
 Dale, 84513, (435)381–2404

Veterinarian: Animal Hospital, 1989 E. Airport RD., Price,
 84501, (435) 637–5797

Hospitals: Castle View Hospital, 300 N. Hospital Dr., Price,
 84501, (435) 637–4800

Gov Agency: BUREAU   OF   LAND   MANAGEMENT
 Field Office - Price, 125 South 600 West, Price, 84501,
 (435) 636–3600

Other comments: The trail goes beyond the ten miles out as
 listed above. This would be a great area for a pack trip
 and dispersed camping.

Typical vegetation and scenery along the San Rafael River.

LOAFER MOUNTAIN TRAIL
TO SANTAQUIN PEAK

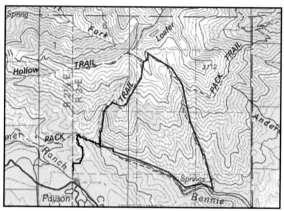

The Loafer Mountain trail climbs above the tree line.
From there Provo, Thistle and many other areas can be viewed.

Topo Map: Birdseye, #39111-H5-TF-024
Name of Trailhead: Loafer Mountain
Name of Trail: Loafer Mountain Trail to Santaquin Peak
Trail #: 098
Property of: UNITED STATES FOREST SERVICE
Other Trails used by this route: Deer Hollow - #112, Bennie Creek - #071
Connecting Trails: Blackhawk - #084
Directions from the closest town to trailhead: Take I-15 to Payson on Highway 6. Travel east on East 700 South Street and follow it about 2 blocks until it turns south on Canyon Road. Follow Canyon Road up Payson Canyon approximately 9 miles, just north of Payson Lakes. The trailhead is a fenced, graveled parking area on the east side of the road.
Road Conditions: The road is steep with many sharp turns. The drive to the trailhead is slow going for a vehicle towing a trailer. The road is closed during the winter

months.

Parking instructions: There is plenty of dispersed parking; park anywhere.

Parking capacity: 20 Trucks and Trailers

Direction of trail from parking area: The trail leaves the parking lot on the north/northeast.

Elevation at T/H: 7,640
Highest Elevation: 9,940
Steepest Grade: 24%
GPS T/H Longitude: 111°38′ 29.09″W
GPS T/H Latitude: 39°56′ 26.80″N
Number of feet Climbing: 3,770

Camping and use restrictions at trailhead and along route: Water for Stock, Weed Free Hay, Camping at T/H, Dispersed Camping

Difficulty: Difficult

To complete this route, horses need to be: Very Fit.

Trail Route & Directions: From the trailhead travel north, crossing the Blackhawk trail at 1/10th of a mile. Then cross the Bennie Creek Trail at about one mile. The trail intersects the Deer Hollow Trail in another 5 miles. Take the Deer Hollow trail back to the Bennie Creek Trail 2 miles, and then on to the Loafer Mountain trail another 2 miles. From there, go back to the trailhead.

General description of route: The trail crosses a stream just before the Blackhawk trail and continues on a gradual incline before intersecting the Bennie Creek Trail. The Loafer Mountain Trail becomes very steep, gaining 2,000 feet over the next five miles. The Deer Hollow trail is not well traveled or maintained, and may be challenging to find at times. The route is especially beautiful as it passes through numerous pockets of maple and Quaken aspen. At the Loafer Mountain ridge is the tree line, and there are some beautiful views.

Type of Route: Loop
Length of Route in Miles: 9.5
Estimated travel time: 4.5 Hours
Route Attractions: Scenery, Campsites and Cell Phone Accessible.
Other Attractions: Beautiful views of Utah County, Mount Nebo, Payson Lakes, Blackhawk and the surrounding country.

Normal Temperatures during
recommended months of use:
Summer: Mild to Hot
Fall: Mild to Cold
Months of Accessibility: June to November

Predominant trail surface: Gravel, Dirt, Loose Rock
Hazards: Steep Sections of Trail, Narrow Trail with Steep Drop-offs
Description of Hazards: Loafer Mountain is steep. It is advised to take a well-conditioned horse.

Current Level Of Use:
(High - greater than 7 in group; Low - 3 or less.)
Horsemen: Low
Motorized: Seldom
Bicyclists: Seldom
Hikers: Low

Tack & Equipment Dealers: Broken Spoke Tack Shop, 898 E 100 North, PAYSON, 84651 - 2347, (801) 465–0904
Police: Utah County Sheriff, 3075 North Main, Spanish Fork, 84660, (801)851–4000

Veterinarian: West Mountain Veterinary Hosp, 143 W 900 North, PAYSON, 84651, (801) 465–4648

Hospitals: Utah Valley Regional MED Center, 1034 N 500 W, Provo, 84604, (801) 357–7056

Gov Agency: Uinta National Forest, 88 West 100 North, Provo, 84601, (801) 342–5100

Other comments: There is very little water after crossing Bennie Creek; take plenty with you. The upper parts of the trail are usually covered with some snow from mid-November through late June. Call the Spanish Fork Ranger Dist. for information, (801) 789–3571.

LOWER MULEY TWIST FROM THE POST

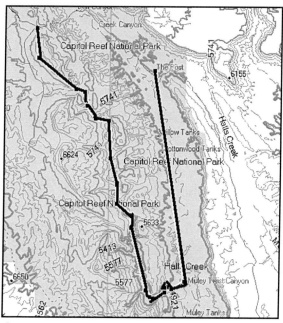

Lower Muley Twist canyon is breathtaking. Take a camera.
The name comes from the narrows, "narrow enough to make mule twist".

Topo Map: The Post, #37110-G8-TF024 and Wagon Box
    Mesa, #37111-G1-TF-024

Name of Trailhead: The Post

Name of Trail: Lower Muley Twist from The Post

Property of: National Parks

Other Trails used by this route: Grand Gulch

Connecting Trails: Upper Muley Twist, Halls Creek
    Cutoff

Directions from the closest town to trailhead: Turn south
    on the Notum Road, which is 20 miles east of Torrey.
    Follow the road about 32 miles to the Burr Trail. Turn
    west on the Burr Trail and travel about 2.25 miles to
    the dispersed trailhead, or continue on to The Post cor-

rals, about 3 miles.

Road Conditions: From Torrey, the road is paved to the Notum Road. Portions of the Notum road are also paved, but most of it is graded dirt. Travel the dirt road with caution in wet weather.

Parking instructions: Both trailheads are dispersed parking.

Parking capacity: 20 Trucks and Trailers

Direction of trail from parking area: Both trails leave the areas from the south.

Elevation at T/H: 4,870
Highest Elevation: 5,390
Steepest Grade: 17%
GPS T/H Longitude: 110°58′ 54.73″W
GPS T/H Latitude: 37°50′ 0.36″N
Number of feet Climbing: 810

Camping and use restrictions at trailhead and along route: Water For Stock, Primitive Camping, Weed Free Hay, Camping at T/H, Dispersed Camping

Other Restrictions: Most of the Muley Twist is in Capital Reef National Park. Follow the park rules and restrictions. Stock water can be found in the "tanks" as is indicated on most maps.

Difficulty: Moderate

To complete this route, horses need to be: Moderately Fit.

Trail Route & Directions: From The Post, follow the Grand Gulch about 2.75 miles to the mouth of Muley Twist Canyon. Follow the canyon West/Northwest to the Burr Trail. The trail could be a loop by following the Cutoff Trail. However, the Cutoff Trail is very steep.

General description of route: The canyon runs within the Waterpocket Fold. It has varied spectacular scenery including narrows, arches, and panoramic views of the fold.

Type of Route: Out and Back.
Length of Route in Miles: 23.5
Estimated travel time: 9.5 Hours
Route Attractions: Scenery, Campsites and Restrooms.
Other Attractions: A short distance from the mouth of the canyon is a large, cave-like arch, which makes a great rest stop.

Normal Temperatures during recommended months of use:
Winter: Cold
Spring: Mild to Cold
Fall: Mild to Cold
Months of Accessibility: September to April

Predominant trail surface: Sand, Gravel, Rock, Dirt
Hazards: Slick Rock, Rock Slides, Steep Sections of Trail, Narrow Trail with Steep Drop-offs
Description of Hazards : Plan ahead! This area has very little water for stock or humans. Be prepared for harsh weather conditions and rough terrain.

Current Level of Use:
(High - greater than 7 in group; Low - 3 or less.)
Horsemen: Seldom
Motorized: None
Bicyclists: Seldom
Hikers: Low

Tack & Equipment Dealers: JS 2 Tack & Saddlery, 75 E. Main, Wellington, (435) 637–4428
Police: WAYNE COUNTY SHERIFF, Wayne County Courthouse, Loa, 84747, (435)836–2789

Veterinarian: Tri County Veterinary Hospital, 352 E. 200 N., Torrey, (435) 425–3487

Hospitals: IHC (Richfield), 1000 N. Main, Venice, . 84701, (435) 896–8271

Gov Agency: Capital Reef National Park, HC 70 Box 15, Torrey, 84775 (435) 425–3791

Other comments: Nature can alter conditions drastically. Go prepared for almost anything. Contact the park staff for current road, trail, feed, and water conditions. Carry plenty of water and drink it. Carry at least one gallon per person and fifteen gallons per horse per day. Flash floods are possible.

Lower Muley Twist, looking south down the canyon.

MIDDLE FORK

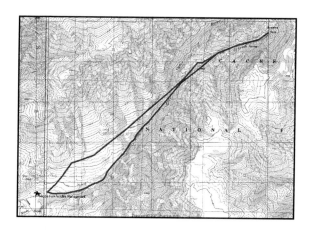

Topo Map: Browns Hole - #4111-C6-TF-024
Name of Trailhead (T/H): Middle Fork Wildlife
 Management Area
Name of Trail: Middle Fork
Property of: USFS
Directions from the closest town to trailhead: Travel to
 Hanksville on highway 39 (about 9 miles form I-15
 in Ogden). By-pass Hanksville and follow the road to
 where it forks with 7800 East. Follow 7800 East to
 Middle Fork Wild Life Management area in the north-
 east portion of the valley.
Road Conditions: It is a two lane paved highway to the
 campground.
Parking instructions: Park anywhere in the campground.
Parking capacity: 20 Trucks and Trailers
Direction of trail from parking area: Northeast of the
 parking/camping area.

Elevation at T/H: 5,035
Highest Elevation: 6,630

Steepest Grade: 13%
GPS T/H Longitude: 111°45′ 17″W
GPS T/H Latitude: 41°17′ 7″N
Number of feet Climbing: 1,925

Camping and use restrictions at trailhead and along route: Water For Stock, Weed Free Hay, Camping at Trailhead

Other Restrictions: Dry Camping only. The outhouse is functional but needs repair. Tie stalls are available with feed boxes.

Difficulty: Moderate

To complete this route, horses need to be: Moderately Fit.

Trail Route & Directions: There are many trails in the area. A favorite is the trail along the Ogden River to Browns Hole and back along the power line road. The trail starts out at the northeast of the parking/ camping area. There is a green gate at the beginning of the trail. Follow the trail right to follow the Ogden River. Follow the trail a little less than 2 miles to a split. Keep right to cross the river. There is a small wood shed and fire ring in the middle of a fork in the river called the bus stop. From there, take the power line road to Browns Hole (or continue to follow the trail along the river). Follow the power line road back to the trailhead.

General description of route: It is rugged forested country with plenty of water and rocks. The area is managed for mule deer and other big game.

Type of Route: Out and Back

Length of Route in Miles: 9

Estimated travel time: 3.5 Hours

Route Attractions: Scenery, Campsites.

**Normal Temperatures during
recommended months of use:**
Spring: Cool To Cold
Summer: Cool to Hot
Fall: Cool to Cold
Months of Accessibility: Open on
May 15th through November.

Predominant trail surface: Rock, Jeep Trail, Dirt, Loose Rock

Hazards: Deep or Wide Water Crossings, Steep Sections of Trail

Description of Hazards: River crossing and mud on the lower trail. Water levels in the river can be high in the spring, and the upper power line trail is rocky.

Current Level Of Use:
(High - greater than 7 in group; Low - 3 or less.)
Horsemen: Moderate
Motorized: None
Bicyclists: Low
Hikers: Low

Tack & Equipment Dealers: Dee's Tire & Farm Supply, 1845 S. Morgan Valley Dr., Morgan, 84050, 801–829–6523

Police: WEBER COUNTY SHERIFF, 457 26th Street, Ogden, 84401, (801)399–8183

Veterinarian: Mountain States Equine, 7283 W. 900 S., Ogden, (801) 731–4244

Hospitals: MaKay-Dee Hospital, 4401 Harrison Boulevard, Ogden, 84403, 801–627–2800

Gov Agency: Wasatch-Cache National Forest, 125 South State Street, Salt Lake City, 84138, (801) 236–3400

MILL CANYON TRAIL TO THE TIBBLE FORK TRAIL

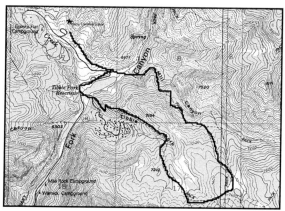

The Mill Canyon trail starts on the north end of Tibble Fork Reservoir, returning on the Tibble Fork Trail.

Topo Map: Timpanogas Cave, # 40111-D5-TF-024

Name of Trailhead: Horse Transfer Station

Name of Trail: Mill Canyon Trail to the Tibble Fork Trail

    Trail #: 040

Property of: UNITED STATES FOREST SERVICE

Other Trails used by this route: Tibble Fork - #041

Connecting Trails: Ridge Trail - #157, Mud Springs Trail - #173, Holman's Ridge Cabin Flat Trail - #172

Directions from the closest town to trailhead: From Alpine & Highland, travel east to on Highway 92 to American Fork Canyon. Go five miles up the canyon and turn north at the Tibble Fork Reservoir sign. Continue two and half miles to the north end of Tibble Fork Lake and, staying on the paved road, go west 1/2 mile to "Horse Transfer Station" trailhead on the right side of the road.

Road Conditions: Highway 92 is narrow but well maintained. Use caution when passing the Timpanogas

National Park; 20 miles per hour is the speed limit in park.

Parking instructions: The parking lot is large. Most people parallel park.

Parking capacity: 20 Trucks and Trailers

Direction of trail from parking area: It's in the southeast corner of parking lot. A little south of the picnic area is the trail, leading east.

Elevation at T/H: 6,361
Highest Elevation: 7,427
Steepest Grade: 20%
GPS T/H Longitude: 111°38′ 57.17″W
GPS T/H Latitude: 40°29′ 17.94″N
Number of feet Climbing: 1,574

Camping and use restrictions at trailhead and along route: Water For Stock, Potable Water, Truck Unloading Ramp, Primitive Camping, Weed Free Hay

Other Restrictions: No camping is allowed by the Forest Service at the trailhead.

Difficulty: Moderate

To complete this route, horses need to be: Moderately Fit

Trail Route & Directions: The trail leaves the parking lot on the southeast, going back to Tibble Fork Lake. Cross the gravel road and pick up the trail about 50 feet north. Cross the stream at the north of the lake and pick up the Mill Canyon trail going east. It is uphill about 2 miles to the meadow with the old beaver dam on the left. Follow the trail as it turns south to the Tibble Fork Trail. Follow the Tibble Fork Trail back to the dam.

General description of route: The Mill Canyon Trail is wide and follows an old roadway that the forest has grown over, to the meadow that is used as the crossover point to the Tibble Fork Trail. The Ponderosa pine, Douglas

Fir, spruce, white fir, and aspen lined trail is uphill to the meadow of mixed grasses. From the meadow to the Tibble Fork it is relatively flat. The return trail is downhill and crosses the Tibble Fork dam.

Type of Route: Loop

Length of Route in Miles: 4.25

Estimated travel time: 2.5 Hours

Route Attractions: Scenery, Fishing, Conditioning, Drinking Water, Showers, RV Facilities, Campsites, Restrooms and Provisions for horses.

Other Attractions: There is an unloading dock for truck loaded horses. Wildlife includes mule deer, elk, moose, mountain goats, black bear, coyote, badgers, weasels, foxes and flying squirrels.

Normal Temperatures during recommended months of use:

Spring: Cool to Mild

Summer: Mild to Hot

Fall: Mild to Cold

Months of Accessibility: Late April (snow permitting) to late October.

Predominant trail surface: Jeep Trail, Dirt, Loose Rock

Hazards: Deep or Wide Water Crossings, Steep Sections of Trail, Busy Road Crossings

Description of Hazards: The trail crosses a dirt road by Tibble Fork Lake. This road is frequently used by four wheelers and OHVs.

Current Level of Use:
(High - greater than 7 in group; Low - 3 or less.)

Horsemen: Moderate

Motorized: Low

Bicyclists: Low

Hikers: Seldom

Tack & Equipment Dealers: Highland IFA Country Stores, 521 W 200 North, HIGHLAND, 84003 (801) 756–9604

Police: UTAH COUNTY SHERIFF, Provo, 84603, (801)343–4001

Veterinarian: South Valley Large Animal Clinic, 1791 W 11400 South, SOUTH JORDAN, 84095, (801) 254–2333

Hospitals: Utah Valley Regional MED Center, 1034 N 500 W, Provo, 84604, (801) 357–7056

Gov Agency: Uinta National Forest, 88 West 100 North, Provo, 84601, (801) 342–5100

Other comments: Weather conditions change quickly. Be prepared for sun, wind, cold, and hot weather.

MILL CANYON TO MUD SPRINGS

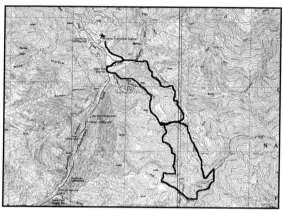

*The figure 8 loop from Tibble Fork reservoir to the Mud Springs
trail to the Ridge Trail. Watch for Moose around the beaver ponds.*

Topo Map: Timpanogas Cave, # 40111-D5-TF-024
Name of Trailhead: Horse Transfer Station
Name of Trail: Mill Canyon Trail
Trail #: '040 to '041
Property of: UNITED STATES FOREST SERVICE
Other Trails used by this route: Tibble Fork - #041, Mud
    Spring Trail -#173, Ridge Trial, #157
Connecting Trails: Holman Ridge Cabin Flat Trail - #173
Directions from the closest town to trailhead: From Alpine
    & Highland, travel east to on Highway 92 to American
    Fork Canyon. Go five miles up the canyon and turn
    north at the Tibble Fork Reservoir sign. Continue two
    and half miles to the north end of Tibble Fork Lake
    and, staying on the paved road, go west 1/2 mile to
    "Horse Transfer Station" trailhead on the right side of
    the road.
Road Conditions: Highway 92 is narrow but well main-
    tained. Use caution when passing the Timpanogas
    National Park. It is 20 miles per hour in the park.

Parking instructions: The parking lot is large. Most people parallel park.

Parking capacity: 20 Trucks and Trailers

Direction of trail from parking area: South east corner of parking lot.

Elevation at T/H: 6,361
Highest Elevation: 8,278
Steepest Grade: 21%
GPS T/H Longitude: 111°38′ 57.17″W
GPS T/H Latitude: 40°29′ 17.4″N
Number of feet Climbing: 3,270

Camping and use restrictions at trailhead and along route: Water For Stock, Potable Water, Truck Unloading Ramp, Primitive Camping, Weed Free Hay

Other Restrictions: No camping at trailhead.

Difficulty: Moderate

To complete this route, horses need to be: Moderately Fit

Trail Route & Directions: The trail leaves the parking lot on the southeast, going back to Tibble Fork Lake. Cross the gravel road and pick up the trail about 50 feet north. Cross the stream at the north of the lake and pick up the Mill Canyon trail going east. Travel uphill about 2 miles to the meadow with the old beaver dam on the left. Follow the trail as it turns south to the Tibble Fork Trail, about a quarter mile. At the junction, cross the Tibble Fork trail to the Mud Springs trail, #173. At the meadow that looks over the Timpanogas Wilderness area, the trail turns east. At the junction, pick up the Ridge Trail, #157, and follow it north to the Tibble Fork trail, #041. The Tibble Fork trail will take you back to the Tibble Fork dam and back to the trailhead.

General description of route: The trail is tree covered and uphill to the meadow. From the meadow to the Tibble Fork is relatively flat. The Mud Spring trail is steep and ends in a meadow with some old water troughs. The Ridge Trail winds northward to the Tibble Fork Trail. Most of the route is tree covered. Great views of the Lone Peak, Timpanogas Wilderness and Heber City areas can be seen from the numerous meadows along the way.

Type of Route: Loop

Length of Route in Miles: 7.5

Estimated travel time: 3.5 Hours

Route Attractions: Scenery, Fishing, Conditioning, Drinking Water, RV Facilities, Campsites, Restrooms and Provisions for horses.

Other Attractions: There is an unloading dock for truck loaded horses. Wildlife includes mule deer, elk, moose, mountain goats, black bear, coyote, badgers, weasels, foxes, and flying squirrels.

**Normal Temperatures during
recommended months of use:**
Spring: Cool to Mild
Summer: Mild to Hot
Fall: Mild to Cold
Months of Accessibility: Late April
(snow permitting) to late October.

Predominant trail surface: Sand, Gravel, Rock, Jeep Trail, Dirt, Loose Rock

Hazards: Deep or Wide Water Crossings, Bogs, Steep Sections of Trail, Busy Road Crossings

Description of Hazards : The trail crosses a dirt road by Tibble Fork Lake, which is frequently used by four wheelers and OHVs.

Current Level of Use:
(High - greater than 7 in group; Low - 3 or less.)
Horsemen: Moderate
Motorized: Allowed on portions
Bicyclists: Not Allowed
Hikers: Seldom

Tack & Equipment Dealers: Highland IFA Country Stores, 521 W 200 North, HIGHLAND, 84003 (801) 756–9604

Police: Utah County Sheriff, 3075 North Main, Spanish Fork, 84660, (801)851–4000

Veterinarian: South Valley Large Animal Clinic, 1791 W 11400 South, SOUTH JORDAN, 84095, (801) 254–2333

Hospitals: Utah Valley Regional MED Center, 1034 N 500 W, Provo, 84604, (801) 357–7056

Gov Agency: Uinta National Forest, 88 West 100 North, Provo, 84601, (801) 342–5100

Other comments: Weather conditions change quickly. Be prepared for sun, wind, cold, and hot weather. The area was used as a camp for the CCCs during the great depression era. Many of the roads and landscape changes can be attributed to the CCC activities.

MOUNTAIN VIEW TRAIL, SALT LAKE COUNTY

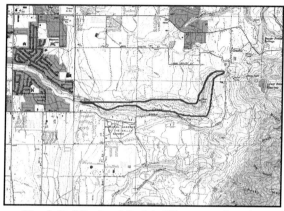

Dimple Dell Regional Park is 680 acres and reaches from 3rd East to Dimple Dell Road (3000 east).

Topo Map: Draper, # 40111-E7-TF-024
Name of Trailhead: Wrangler Trailhead, Dimple Dell
Name of Trail: Mountain View Trail, Salt Lake County
Property of: Salt Lake County
Other Trails used by this route: North Rim View Trail
Connecting Trails: Sleepy Hollow, Fox Hollow, North Rim, Fox Trail, Mountain View Trail, and many more.
Directions from the closest town to trailhead: In Sandy City, go to 1300 East and 10600 South. Just north of 10600 South, turn east to the parking area on the north side of the wash.
Road Conditions: City and state maintained roads.
Parking instructions: Trailhead parking is on the north side of the wash. 45° parking.
Parking capacity: 10 Trucks and Trailers
Direction of trail from parking area: The trail is east of the trailhead, past the truck/stock unloading ramp and tie rails.

Elevation at T/H: 4,600
Highest Elevation: 5,100
Steepest Grade: 6%
GPS T/H Longitude: 111°48' 5.21"W
GPS T/H Latitude: 040°33' 41.94"N
Number of feet Climbing: 400

Camping and use restrictions at trailhead and along route: Water For Stock, Potable Water, Truck Unloading Ramp

Other Restrictions: No camping, pets must be on leash.

Difficulty: Easy

To complete this route, horses need to be: Sound Only

Trail Route & Directions: Follow the trail east from the trailhead and drop down into the wash about a 1/16 of a mile. Follow one of the many trails east.

General description of route: The trail follows a wash east through Cottonwood trees and brush. At the east end, follow the route north around the small reservoir. At the northeast corner, the trail winds up a small gully as it turns west and comes out on at the top of the canyon. Follow the trail along the rim, or one of the many other trails, to return to the trailhead.

Type of Route: Loop

Length of Route in Miles: 6.4 Miles

Estimated travel time: 2 Hours

Route Attractions: Scenery, Conditioning, Drinking Water, Cell Phone Accessible, Restrooms and Provisions for horses.

Other Attractions: Great for conditioning.

**Normal Temperatures during
recommended months of use:**
Winter: Mild to Cold
Spring: Mild to Warm

Summer: Hot
Fall: Mild to Warm

Months of Accessibility: Year round, summer can be hot.

Predominant trail surface: Sand, Jeep Trail, Dirt
Other surfaces: There are wood chips along some of the wider corridors.
Hazards: Busy Road Crossings.
Description of Hazards: The west portion of park can be accessed by crossing the very busy 1300 east.

Current Level of Use:
(High - greater than 7 in group; Low - 3 or less.)
Horsemen: Moderate
Motorized: Not Allowed
Bicyclists: Low
Hikers: Low

Tack & Equipment Dealers: Saddle Up, 11415 S Redwood Rd, SOUTH JORDAN, 84095 - 7804, (801) 254–5700
Police: Sandy Police Department, 142 Main St, Sandy, (801) 255–8914
Veterinarian: South Valley Large Animal Clinic, 1791 W 11400 South, SOUTH JORDAN, 84095, (801) 254–2333
Hospitals: Alta View Hospital, 9660 S 1300 E, Sandy, 84094, (801) 501–2600
Gov Agency: Salt Lake County Parks and Rec. Adm., 2001 South State Street S4400, Salt Lake City, 84190, (801)483–5473
Other comments: This county, open space park is great winter, spring, and fall riding. It is very good conditioning for horses that have not been ridden for awhile

or training. The park offers all kinds of terrain, so it is great for training opportunities.

The Wrangler Trailhead at 1300 East and 10400 South in Sandy.

NINE MILE

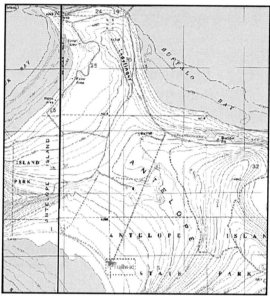

This map shows the road to the trail head. The trail takes off from the east of the parking area.

Topo Map: Antelope Island N, # 41112-A2-TF-024
Name of Trailhead: Antelope Island
Name of Trail: Nine Mile
Property of: Utah State Parks
Connecting Trails: Elephant Point.
Directions from the closest town to trailhead: From I-15, take exit 335 or Antelope Drive west to the island. Once on the island, travel south and follow the road southwest past the visitors center. Turn east on the road towards the buffalo corrals. Turn south on the first dirt road and follow it to the turn east.
Road Conditions: There are state and local maintained roads that are passable year round.
Parking instructions: No formal parking markers can be found at this parking lot. Most park on a 45° angle to

allow an easy exit from the parking lot.

Parking capacity: 20 Trucks and Trailers

Direction of trail from parking area: The trail is on the southeast corner of the parking lot, through the chain link fence.

Elevation at T/H: 4,553

Highest Elevation: 4,895

Steepest Grade: 7%

GPS T/H Longitude: 112°14′ 27.52″W

GPS T/H Latitude: 041°01′ 25.80″N

Number of feet Climbing: 227

Camping and use restrictions at trailhead and along route: Weed Free Hay, Camping at T/H

Other Restrictions: The terrain is very fragile due to the thin topsoil. All users must stay on the established trails.

Difficulty: Easy

To complete this route, horses need to be: Sound Only

Trail Route & Directions: The route from the parking lot turns northeast up the foothills and circles back to the trailhead. Because the terrain on the island is very thin topsoil, park rules state that all trail users must stay on the trails.

General description of route: The trail is sandy with some rocks. The trail is in open desert country, with very little tree cover. The route, if followed from the northeast, runs up over the foothills for a view of the Wasatch Front Mountains, cities, and the eastern parts of the Great Salt Lake. The trail follows the skyline south, through a saddle, and back down a wide open valley. At the west end of the valley, the trail returns northwest to the parking lot.

Type of Route: Loop

Length of Route in Miles: 9.5 miles

Estimated travel time: 3 Hours

Route Attractions: Scenery, Conditioning, Drinking Water, RV Facilities, Campsites and Cell Phone Accessible.

Other Attractions: Antelope Island is home to a large bison herd, pronghorn, mule deer, numerous bird species, and a lot of other wildlife.

Normal Temperatures during recommended months of use:
Winter: Cool to Cold
Spring: Mild to Cold
Fall: Mild to Cold
Months of Accessibility: Fall to Spring

Predominant trail surface: Sand, Gravel, Rock, Jeep Trail

Description of Hazards: The bison are numerous and dangerous when provoked. While it is required that users stay on the trails, do not stay on them if the buffalo are on them. Find a route around them. On a short sprint, a bison can outrun a horse, so do not get too close.

Current Level of Use:
(High - greater than 7 in group; Low - 3 or less.)
Horsemen: High
Motorized: Not Allowed
Bicyclists: High
Hikers: Moderate

Tack & Equipment Dealers: A. A. Callister Corp, 3615 S Redwood Rd, West Valley City, 84119, (801) 973–7058

Police: DAVIS COUNTY SHERIFF, 800 West State St., Farmington, 84025, (801)451–4120

Veterinarian: Clearfield Veterinary Clinic, 428 N. Main, Clearfield, (801) 776–4372

Hospitals: South Davis Community Hospital, 401 S 400 E, Bountiful, 84010, (801) 295–2361

Gov Agency: Antelope Island State Park 4528 W 1700 South Syracuse Entrance Station, (801) 773–2941

Viewing the numerous bison south of the old historic GarrRanch.

NORTH OF SNOW CANYON, ST. GEORGE

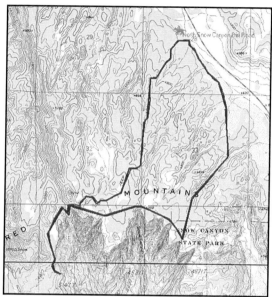

The brim of Snow Canyon is craggy and offers beautiful views of the area.

Topo Map: Veyo, #37113-C6-TF-024
Name of Trailhead: North of Snow Canyon
Name of Trail: North of Snow Canyon, St. George
Property of: BUREAU OF LAND MANAGEMENT
Directions from the closest town to trailhead: On the west side of St. George, travel north on Highway 18, 13.5 miles from the junction of highway's 34 and 18. The trailhead is on the left side (southeast) of the road.
Road Conditions: Highway 18 is a paved, two lane, well maintained highway.
Parking instructions: Park just off the highway in the cedars.
Parking capacity: 20 Trucks and Trailers
Direction of trail from parking area: Follow the jeep road east/southeast.

Elevation at T/H: 4,780
Highest Elevation: 5,157
Steepest Grade: 18%
GPS T/H Longitude: 113°39′ 6.48″W
GPS T/H Latitude: 37°16′ 48.29″N
Number of feet Climbing: 1330

Camping and use restrictions at trailhead and along route: Weed Free Hay, Camping at T/H
Difficulty: Easy
To complete this route, horses need to be: Sound Only
Trail Route & Directions: Most of the route is a jeep trail. Travel the road southeast as it follows the rise in terrain. Follow the road to the brim of Snow Canyon State Park. Ride west along the brim until it meets the jeep trail on the west side. For a great view of the canyon, follow the road south along the ridge. Double back along the road and follow it back to the trailhead.
General description of route: The route is a jeep road traveling through the desert, lined with cedar trees and red rock country. The view from the rim of Snow Canyon is spectacular. To the east, another trail running into the canyon can be seen.
Type of Route: Loop
Length of Route in Miles: 8
Estimated travel time: 2.5 Hours
Route Attractions: Scenery, Conditioning Campsites and Cell Phone Accessible.
Other Attractions: It is very easy traveling along this route. It is great for conditioning or a leisurely ride with great views.

Normal Temperatures during recommended months of use:
Winter: Cool to Cold
Spring: Cool to Warm
Summer: Hot
Fall: Warm to Cool
Months of Accessibility: Year round

Predominant trail surface: Sand, Gravel, Rock, Jeep Trail
Hazards: Slick Rock
Description of Hazards: Jeep road most of the trail.

Current Level Of Use:
(High - greater than 7 in group; Low - 3 or less.)
Horsemen: Low
Motorized: Low
Bicyclists: Seldom
Hikers: Seldom

Tack & Equipment Dealers: Holyoak Saddles, 287 N. Bluff, St. George, (435) 673–9548

Police: WASHINGTON COUNTY SHERIFF, 750 South 5400 West, Hurricane, 84737, (435)656–6601

Veterinarian: Virgin River Veterinary Clinic, 525 W State St, Hurricane, (435) 635–4161

Hospitals: River Road IHC Health Center, 577 S. River Road, St. George, 84790, (435) 688–6100

Gov Agency: BUREAU OF LAND MANAGEMENT Field Office - Cedar City, 176 East D.L. Sergeant Drive, Cedar City, 84720, (435) 586–2401

Other comments: There is no water in the area for stock. Depending on the weather conditions, you may want to carry water.

NORTH WILLOW TRAIL, STANSBURY MOUNTAINS

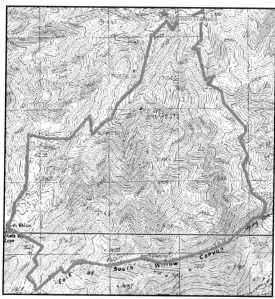

*North Willow climbs to the Deseret Peak Wilderness, passes
North and South Willow Lakes. The Miners Fork
Route back is steep going most of the way.*

Topo Map: Deseret Peak East, # 40112-D5-TF-024
Name of Trailhead: O.P. Miller Campground
Name of Trail: North Willow Trail, Stansbury Mountains
Trail #: 036
Property of: UNITED STATES FOREST SERVICE
Other Trails used by this route: Mining Fork and Front
    Trail - #031
Connecting Trails: Pass Canyon - #034
Directions from the closest town to trailhead: From
    highway 40 (Main Street of Grantsville), turn south
    on Cooley's Lane. Look for the Forest Service sign.
    Follow the road south to the sign indicating North

Willow Canyon, about one mile. Turn west on the dirt road and follow the road towards Davenport Canyon for about three miles. Take the road southwest towards North Willow Canyon. It is another four miles to the O.P. Miller Campground.

Road Conditions: Roads include I-80 to Grantsville, a two lane highway to and from Grantsville, and a dirt road to the North Willow campground. The dirt road is usually graded and passable, but may be very muddy and slippery when wet.

Parking instructions: Parking is available at the campground and the surrounding area.

Parking capacity: 7 Trucks and Trailers

Direction of trail from parking area: The trail can be found by traveling west on the road out of the campground.

Elevation at T/H: 6,500
Highest Elevation: 8,950
Steepest Grade: 17%
GPS T/H Longitude: 112°35' 46.61"W
GPS T/H Latitude: 40°31' 37.85"N
Number of feet Climbing: 2,784

Camping and use restrictions at trailhead and along route: Water for Stock, Potable Water, Primitive Camping, Weed Free Hay, Camping at T/H

Other Restrictions: Much of the trail is in a wilderness area and is restricted to wilderness uses.

Difficulty: Moderate

To complete this route, horses need to be: Moderately Fit

Trail Route & Directions: The trail can be found by traveling 1/2 mile west on the road out of the campground. There are two routes at the end of the road; keep to the right (north). The other trail dead ends. The four wheel road turns into a trail about 1.25 miles from the campground. The trail continues traveling south/southwest just below North Willow Lake and over the ridge to the Mining Fork Trail. Follow the Mining Fork Trail east to the Front Trail. Following the Front Trail north, the route rejoins the road just east of the trailhead and campground.

General description of route: The route starts out on a dirt road or four wheel track, crossing the stream several times, and travels southwest along a brushy trail. As the trail turns a little more to the south the route travels through Quaken Aspen, Douglas Fir, Pinyon Pine, Mountain Mahogany, and Juniper Trees.

Type of Route: Loop

Length of Route in Miles: 9

Estimated travel time: 4.5 Hours

Route Attractions: Scenery, Fishing, Drinking Water and Campsite.

Other Attractions: Lots of wildlife and normally very few travelers are in the area. Especially abundant is the mule deer population. Much of the area is in the Deseret Peak Wilderness, which prohibits mechanical travel.

Normal Temperatures during recommended months of use:

Spring: Mild to Cold

Summer: Mild to Hot

Fall: Mild to Cool

Months of Accessibility: June to October

Predominant trail surface: Sand, Gravel, Rock, Jeep Trail, Dirt, Loose Rock

Hazards: Bogs, Steep Sections of Trail, Narrow Trail with Steep Drop-offs

Description of Hazards: Some of the trail is not well traveled and may be brushy. There may be deep snow on the higher elevations of the trail through early June.

Current Level of Use:
(High - greater than 7 in group; Low - 3 or less.)
Horsemen: Low
Motorized: Not Allowed
Bicyclists: Not Allowed
Hikers: Seldom

Tack & Equipment Dealers: A. A. Callister Corp, 3615 S Redwood Rd, West Valley City, 84119, (801) 973–7058

Police: TOOELE SHERIFF, 47 S MAIN ST, TOOELE, (435) 665–2228

Veterinarian: Countryside Animal Clinic, 254 S Main St, TOOELE, , (435) 882–4100

Hospitals: Mountain West Medical Center, 2055 N Main, TOOELE, (435) 843–3600

Gov Agency: Wasatch-Cache National Forest, 125 South State Street, Salt Lake City, 84138, (801) 236–3400

Other comments: The view from the top looks out over the Tooele City and the Oquirrh and Wasatch Mountains. The Great Salt Lake and parts of the Wasatch Front can also be seen.

Looking Over the North Willow Trail.

RIGHT HAND FORK OF MAPLE CANYON

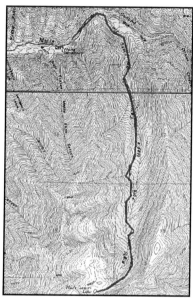

Maple is a beautifully shaded canyon,
great for riding on hot day.

Topo Map: Springville - # 40111-B5-TF-024, Spanish Fork
   Peak - #40111-A5–TF-024

Name of Trailhead : Whiting Campground

Name of Trail: Right Hand Fork of Maple Canyon

Property of: UNITED STATES FOREST SERVICE

Other Trails used by this route: Maple Canyon

Connecting Trails: Sterling Hollow, Mill Hollow

Directions from the closest town to trailhead: At the intersection of highway 147 and East Maple Street, turn
   north and travel to East 400 North Street. Follow the
   street as it winds into Maple Canyon. The trailhead is
   east of the Whiting Campground.

Road Conditions: Paved to the trailhead.

Parking instructions: The parking area is small. Park along
   the sides of the road.

Parking capacity: 5 Trucks and Trailers
Direction of trail from parking area: Travel east along the jeep trail to the trail.

Elevation at T/H: 5,540
Highest Elevation: 8,741
Steepest Grade: 22%
GPS T/H Longitude: 111°31′ 21.55″W
GPS T/H Latitude: 40°8′ 6.99″N
Number of feet Climbing: 3640

Camping and use restrictions at trailhead and along route: Water For Stock, Weed Free Hay, Camping at T/H, Dispersed Camping
Difficulty: Moderate **To complete this route, horses need to be:** Moderately Fit
Trail Route & Directions: Follow the jeep trail about 1/2 mile. At the fork, follow the trail to the south (right). The trail travels south to the tree line and then turns southwest to Maple Canyon Lake.
General description of route: The trail is generally forest covered with Maples, pines, and Quaken aspen. It is a steep route and rises about 2,800 feet in 2 miles.
Type of Route: Out and Back.
Length of Route in Miles: 7
Estimated travel time: 3 Hours
Route Attractions: Scenery, RV Facilities, Campsites and Restrooms.
Other Attractions: The Whiting Campground is situated in a grove, and all of the camps are shaded in the summer. Wildlife includes mule deer, elk, black bear, hawks, turkey vultures and many other species.

Normal Temperatures during recommended months of use:
Spring: Cold to Mild
Summer: Hot
Fall: Hot to Cold
Months of Accessibility: June to November

Predominant trail surface: Gravel, Rock, Jeep Trail, Dirt, Loose Rock
Other surfaces: Creek crossings.
Hazards: Steep Sections of Trail.

Current Level Of Use:
(High - greater than 7 in group; Low - 3 or less.)
Horsemen: Low
Motorized: None
Bicyclists: Seldom
Hikers: Low

Tack & Equipment Dealers: Broken Spoke Tack Shop, 898 E 100 North, PAYSON, 84651 - 2347, (801) 465–0904

Police: Utah County Sheriff, 3075 North Main, Spanish Fork, 84660, (801)851–4000

Veterinarian: West Mountain Veterinary Hosp, 143 W 900 North, PAYSON, 84651, (801) 465–4648

Hospitals: Utah Valley Regional MED Center, 1034 N 500 W, Provo, 84604, (801) 357–7056

Gov Agency: Uinta National Forest, 88 West 100 North, Provo, 84601, (801) 342–5100

Other comments: The trail summits with an overlook of Spanish Fork Canyon and Diamond Fork. By crossing along the ridge generally northeast on a faint trail, a loop can be made by connecting on the Maple Canyon Trail.

ROCK SPRINGS CREEK TO THE PARIA RIVER

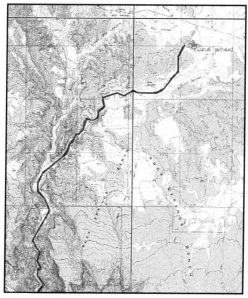

Entering the Paria River via Rock Springs Creek.
The Corral trailhead is at northeast just south of Kodachrome Basin.

Topo Map: Slickrock Bench, #37111-D8-TF-024, Bull Valley Gorge, #37112-D1-TF-024

Name of Trailhead: Corrals south of Kodachrome Basin

Name of Trail: Rock Springs Creek to the Paria River

Property of: BUREAU OF LAND MANAGEMENT

Directions from the closest town to trailhead: Nine miles from Cannonville on the Cottonwood Wash road is Kodachrome Basin State Park. About one mile past the state park is a dirt road on the right (south) side. An old corral is about 1/2 mile down the road. This is a great area to camp if you want to be away from the crowds and have a corral for your stock.

Road Conditions: The road is paved from Cannonville for

the first nine miles, then turns to dirt/clay. The dirt road can be very slick when it is wet.

Parking instructions: There is plenty of room around the corrals area for a lot of rigs.

Parking capacity: 20 Trucks and Trailers

Direction of trail from parking area: Take the dirt road as it crosses the stream about two miles, passing another corral. The trail starts on the north side of the road.

Elevation at T/H: 5,790
Highest Elevation: 5,800
Steepest Grade: 17%
GPS T/H Longitude: 111°58′ 52.88″W
GPS T/H Latitude: 37°29′ 31.77″N
Number of feet Climbing: 224

Camping and use restrictions at trailhead and along route: Water For Stock, Weed Free Hay, Camping at T/H, Dispersed Camping

Difficulty: Easy

To complete this route, horses need to be: Sound Only

Trail Route & Directions: The trail crosses the stream twice more as it drops into a deep gorge. Follow the gorge to the Paria River.

General description of route: The trail starts out on a broad desert wash, sparsely covered with Gambels Oak and Cottonwoods. After about a mile of leaving the road, the route descends into a Navajo Sandstone gorge. The gorge gets narrower and deeper as it progresses towards the Paria River, but is passable.

Type of Route: Out and Back.

Length of Route in Miles: 14

Estimated travel time: 4 Hours

Route Attractions: Scenery, Conditioning, Drinking Water, Showers, RV Facilities, Campsites, Cell Phone Accessible, Restrooms, and Provisions for horses.

Other Attractions: Restrooms, showers and RV Facilities can be found at the Kodachrome Basin campground. There are park and facilities fees.

Normal Temperatures during recommended months of use:
Winter: Cold
Spring: Cold to Mild
Summer: Hot
Fall: Mild to Cool
Months of Accessibility: Early Spring to Late November

Predominant trail surface: Sand, Gravel, Rock, Jeep Trail, Loose Rock
Hazards: Slick Rock, Deep or Wide Water Crossings
Description of Hazards: Watch out for quicksand!! The water has a lot of sediment but is drinkable for stock.

Current Level of Use:
(High - greater than 7 in group; Low - 3 or less.)
Horsemen: Seldom
Motorized: Low
Bicyclists: Seldom
Hikers: Low

Tack & Equipment Dealers: Panguitch Supply, 700 N. Main, Panguitch, (435) 676–2232
Police: SEVIER COUNTY SHERIFF, 835 East 300 North, #200, Richfield, 84701, (435)896–2600
Veterinarian: Kanab Veterinary Hospital, 484 S 100 E, Kanab, (435) 644–2400
Hospitals: Sevier Valley Hospital IHC, 1100 N. Main, Richfield, (435) 896–8271
Gov Agency: BUREAU OF LAND MANAGEMENT Field Office - Grand Staircase NM, 190 E. Center St., Kanab, 84741, (435) 644–4300

Other comments: The weather conditions can change rapidly in this harsh, arid area. Take plenty of water. The canyons along the Paria River have many pictographs and petroglyphs. Near the intersection of the Paria River and Rock Springs Creek is a petroglyph that resembles a bear claw (see the picture). Others can be found in the small canyons along the Paria River. About 20 miles from the trailhead is an old historic movie set that was used to produce Hollywood movies.

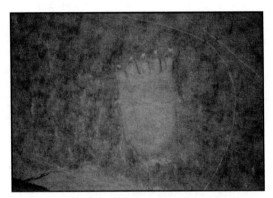

Bear Paw petroglphs at the upper end of the Paria River.

Corrals at Rock Springs Creek.

SETTLEMENT CANYON
OQUIRRH MOUNTAINS

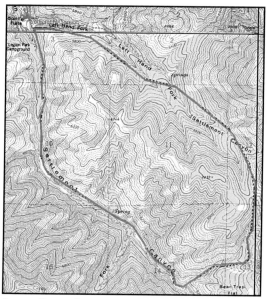

*Settlement Canyon has numerous trails and can be looped back
with varying degrees of difficulty. This route is easy to moderate.*

Topo Map: Tooele - #40112-E1-TF-024, Stockton–#40112-
D3-TF-024, Bingham Canyon– #40112-E2-TF-
024,Lowe Peak–#40112-D4-TF-024

Name of Trailhead: Settlement Canyon

Property of: BUREAU OF LAND MANAGEMENT

Directions from the closest town to trailhead: On highway 36, 1/3rd mile south of the city of Tooele, turn
east (or left if coming from Tooele) on to the paved
road past the reservoir. Travel east to the Spring Flats
Campground on the south of the road. There is plenty
of parking at the campground.

Road Conditions: The road through Tooele County is well
maintained, as is the asphalt road to the trailhead.

Parking instructions: Park at Spring Flats campground.
Parking capacity: 15 Trucks and Trailers
Direction of trail from parking area: The trail is north of
the parking area and across the road entering the area.

Elevation at T/H: 5,446
Highest Elevation: 7,075
Steepest Grade: 14%
GPS T/H Longitude: 112°17′ 15.52″W
GPS T/H Latitude: 40°30′ 4.71″N
Number of feet Climbing: 1,705

**Camping and use restrictions at trailhead and along
route:** Water For Stock, Potable Water, Weed Free
Hay, Camping at T/H
Difficulty: Easy
To complete this route, horses need to be: Sound Only
Trail Route & Directions: The trailhead at the campground
is fenced. Leave the area on the east end. Through the
gates, follow the road back to the main road and cross
it to the north side. Pick up the trail through the scrub
oak and back on to a dirt road. Follow the road a tenth
of a mile to the trail that climbs up the north side of
a wash. Follow the trailup over the ridge and back
down in to the left-hand fork of Settlement Canyon.
The trail comes out west of the dirt road and continues
east/northeast to the pass. Take the route back to a jeep
road. Follow that road east/ south east back down to
Settlement Canyon. By following the road west, the
route returns to the trailhead.
General description of route: The trail is maple and scrub
oak covered for most of the route. Most of the trail
is an easy grade and good for early season conditioning or fall colors. The trail is not rocky and does not
require shod horses. The beginning part of the trail fol-

lows a dirt road.

Type of Route: Loop

Length of Route in Miles: 9

Estimated travel time: 3 Hours

Route Attractions: Scenery, Fishing, Conditioning, Drinking Water, RV Facilities, Campsites and Restrooms.

Other Attractions: The campsite has full RV hookups and livestock corrals. A stream runs on the south side of the campground.

Normal Temperatures during recommended months of use:

Spring: Cool to Mild

Summer: Mild to Hot

Fall: Mild to Cold

Months of Accessibility: April to November

Predominant trail surface: Rock, Jeep Trail, Dirt, Loose Rock

Other surfaces: There is some asphalt road at the beginning of the route.

Hazards: Busy Road Crossings.

Description of Hazards : The return from the left-hand fork is steep along the jeep track.

Current Level of Use:

(High - greater than 7 in group; Low - 3 or less.)

Horsemen: Moderate

Motorized: Seldom

Bicyclists: Seldom

Hikers: Seldom

Tack & Equipment Dealers: A. A. Callister Corp, 3615 S Redwood Rd, West Valley City, 84119, (801) 973–7058

Police: TOOELE SHERIFF, 47 S MAIN ST, TOOELE, ,
(435) 665–2228

Veterinarian: Countryside Animal Clinic, 254 S Main St,
TOOELE, (435) 882–4100

Hospitals: Mountain West Medical Center, 2055 N Main,
TOOELE, (435) 843–3600

Gov Agency: Bureau of Land Management, Utah State
Office, PO Box 45155, Salt Lake City, 84145–0155,
(801) 539–4001

Other comments: There is lots of wildlife, many deer
and elk in the area. This is a fee area (less than $10).
Sometimes they do not charge for day use.

The trail starts in the trees in the background.
This picture looks northeast from the trailhead.

SEVEN MILE CANYON

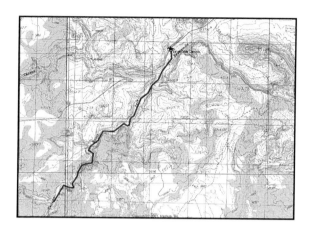

Topo Map: Merrimac Butte - #308109-F6-TF-024
Name of Trailhead (T/H): Seven Mile Canyon
Name of Trail: Seven Mile Canyon
Property of: BLM
Directions from the closest town to trailhead: Take highway 191 north of Moab to Dead Horse Point and turn off. Turn left (west) on . Highway 313. Follow the road to the 3rd pull out with an information kiosk, about 3 miles.
Road Conditions: It is a paved two lane highway from Moab to the pullout.
Parking instructions: Park immediately after pulling off the pavement. Explore before driving down into the camping area.
Parking capacity: 10 Trucks and Trailers
Direction of trail from parking area: Southwest.

Elevation at T/H: 4,600
Highest Elevation: 4,800
Steepest Grade: 12%

GPS T/H Longitude: 109°43′ 28.29″W
GPS T/H Latitude: 38°38′ 52.83″N
Number of feet Climbing: 246

Camping and use restrictions at trailhead and along route: Weed Free Hay, Camping at Trailhead
Other Restrictions: Bring water for stock.
Difficulty: Moderate
To complete this route, horses need to be: Moderately Fit
Trail Route & Directions: Follow the jeep track up the wash. Stay in the main canyon. The side canyons are impassable, and impossible to ride. At the end of the canyon is a pond of water and a great place to picnic.
General description of route: Spectacular rock formations and scenery. It is dry desert country, with possible quick sand in some of the areas around the stream.
Type of Route: Out and Back
Length of Route in Miles: 8
Estimated travel time: 4.5 Hours
Route Attractions: Scenery, Campsites.

Normal Temperatures during recommended months of use:
Winter: Cool to Chilly
Spring: Warm to Cold
Summer: Hot
Fall: Warm to Cool
Months of Accessibility: Fall to Spring

Predominant trail surface: Sand, Gravel, Rock, Jeep Trail
Other surfaces: Shallow water crossings.
Description of Hazards: Shifting Sand, Blind Curves and large vertical pipes in the middle of the trail.

Current Level of Use:
(High - greater than 7 in group; Low - 3 or less.)
Horsemen: Low
Motorized: Moderate
Bicyclists: Low
Hikers: Low

Tack & Equipment Dealers: Spanish Valley Feed Store, 2728 S Hwy 191, (435) 259 6315

Police: Grand County Sheriff - 125 E. Center, Moab, 84532 (435) 259–8115

Veterinarian: Moab Veterinary Clinic, 4575 Spanish Valley Dr, Moab, (435) 259–8710

Hospitals: Allen Memorial Hospital, 719 West Fourth Street, Moab, Tel.1–435–259–7191

Gov Agency: BLM Field Office - Moab, 82 East Dogwood, Moab, 84532, (435) 259–2100

Other comments: Do not go into the area canyons during stormy weather. Flash floods can flow long distances. This canyon drains a large area; flooding is common.

SHINGLE CREEK, UINTA MOUNTAINS

*The Shingle Creek Trailhead from Highway 150, with East Shingle
Lake on the northeast. Most of the trail is tree covered, views
of the creek and many ponds, created by beaver dams.*

Topo Map: Erickson Basin, # 40111-F1-TF-0242
Name of Trailhead: Shingle Creek
Name of Trail: Shingle Creek, Uinta Mountains
Trail #: 069
Property of: UNITED STATES FOREST SERVICE
Connecting Trails: Upper Setting - #156, Lakes Country
 - #066, Erickson Basin - #067
Directions from the closest town to trailhead: From
 Kamas, travel 10 miles east on highway 150. Just
 before the trailhead there is a sign for Shingle Creek
 Campground on the south side of the road. About one
 and a quarter miles farther east on the north side of
 the road is a sign for the trailhead. Turn northeast on
 the road and follow it for about a tenth of a mile to the

trailhead.

Road Conditions: Highway 150 is well maintained road but is closed due to heavy snow during the winter months.

Parking instructions: The trailhead is small with an area on the north side to park several vehicles and trailers. If the trailhead is full, there is a dispersed parking area on the other side of highway 150.

Parking capacity: 5 Trucks and Trailers

Direction of trail from parking area: The trail leaves the parking area on the north. The trail has a stock gate. Leave the gate open or closed as you find it.

Elevation at T/H: 7,660
Highest Elevation: 9,675
Steepest Grade: 26%
GPS T/H Longitude: 111°07′ 13.64″W
GPS T/H Latitude: 40°36′ 29.63″N
Number of feet Climbing: 2,435

Camping and use restrictions at trailhead and along route: Water For Stock, Primitive Camping, Weed Free Hay, Camping at T/H, Dispersed Camping

Difficulty: Moderate

To complete this route, horses need to be: Moderately Fit.

Trail Route & Directions: The trail generally travels north, northeast to East Shingle Creek Lake.

General description of route: The trail is a well established route through a forest of aspens and pines. It is generally a dirt path, but has several rocky areas and crosses the stream in several areas. Near the trailhead there is a bridge that crosses the stream. All of the other crossings parallel small foot bridges.

Type of Route: Out and Back.

Length of Route in Miles: 11

Estimated travel time: 5 Hours

Route Attractions: Scenery, Fishing, Drinking Water and Campsites.

Other Attractions: This trail leads to several other trails, one of which crosses the mountains to Smith and Morehouse Lake above the Weber River. Another trail runs east to the Crystal Lake Trailhead.

Normal Temperatures during recommended months of use:
Summer: Mild to Warm
Fall: Mild to Cold
Months of Accessibility: June to October

Predominant trail surface: Gravel , Rock, Jeep Trail, Dirt, Loose Rock

Hazards: Slick Rock. Deep or Wide Water Crossings, Bogs, Narrow Bridges, Steep Sections of Trail, Narrow Trail with Steep Drop-offs

Description of Hazards: The bridge at the first part of the trail is well maintained and wide enough for a loaded pack horse. There is one section of trail that is steep and has a steep drop-off; however, it is fairly wide and will accommodate pack stock.

Current Level Of Use:
(High - greater than 7 in group; Low - 3 or less.)
Horsemen: Moderate
Motorized: Not Allowed
Bicyclists: None
Hikers: Moderate

Tack & Equipment Dealers: Equus Equestrian Tack & Supply, 6400 N Business Loop Rd, PARK CITY,

(435) 615–7433

Police: SUMMIT COUNTY SHERIFF, 6300 Silver Creek Drive, Park City, 84098, (435)615–3500

Veterinarian: Arcadia Veterinary Clinic, 90 E 1520 N Hwy 40, Heber, (435) 654–0592

Hospitals: Heber Valley Medical Center, 1485 South Highway 40, Heber City, (435) 654–2500

Gov Agency: Uinta National Forest, 88 West 100 North, Provo, 84601, (801) 342–5100

Other comments: In the Uintas, the weather can change drastically in a short period of time. Rain is common on a daily basis. Be prepared for snow, hail, or sleet in summer months.

SMITH & MOREHOUSE TO
SO. ERICKSON LAKE

*The Smith & Morehouse Trail is a gateway to the Lakes
Country and many other trails on the western edge of the Uinta's.*

Topo Map: Erickson Basin, # 40111-F1-TF-024
Name of Trailhead: Ledgefork at Smith & Morehouse
Name of Trail: Smith & Morehouse to So. Erickson Lake
Trail #: 061
Property of: UNITED STATES FOREST SERVICE
Other Trails used by this route: Erickson Basin - #067
Connecting Trails: Lake Country Trail #066, Shingle Creek
   Trail #069
Directions from the closest town to trailhead: 16 miles
   east from Oakley, up the Weber Canyon is Smith &
   Morehouse reservoir. South of the reservoir is the
   Ledgefork Campground. The trailhead is at the south
   end of the campground.

Road Conditions: The highway is paved to the turn off to the reservoir. The last 3.75 miles is a graded dirt road.

Parking instructions: There is a paved parking lot at the trailhead. If it is full, park along the road.

Parking capacity: 20 Trucks and Trailers

Direction of trail from parking area: The trail is at the south end of the parking lot and travels southeast, crossing the Smith & Morehouse Creek.

Elevation at T/H: 7,760
Highest Elevation: 10,099
Steepest Grade: 34%
GPS T/H Longitude: 111°05′ 34.44″W
GPS T/H Latitude: 040°44′ 21.81″N
Number of feet Climbing: 2,630

Camping and use restrictions at trailhead and along route: Water For Stock, Potable Water, Primitive Camping, Weed Free Hay, Camping at T/H, Dispersed Camping

Difficulty: Difficult

To complete this route, horses need to be: Very Fit

Trail Route & Directions: The route leaves the trailhead to the southeast and follows the Smith & Morehouse Trail to the Erickson Basin Trail, from there the route travels south.

General description of route: The route rises slowly along the Smith & Morehouse Trail and then climbs swiftly up the Erickson Basin Trail. The trail is shaded by pines and Quaken Aspen along most of the route. The trail is very rocky and steep along the Erickson Basin Trail. The route crosses the stream several times on both trails. Look for the beaver ponds on the west side of the Smith & Morehouse Trail. The trail crosses some bogs and slick rock in the Erickson Basin.

Type of Route: Out and Back.

Length of Route in Miles: 11

Estimated travel time: 4 Hours

Route Attractions: Scenery, Fishing, Drinking Water, Campsites and Restrooms.

Other Attractions: The canyon has beautiful steep mountains on both sides of the route. It also has lots of wildlife, including moose, elk, mule deer and black bears.

Normal Temperatures during recommended months of use:
Summer: Cool to Hot

Fall: Cool to Cold

Months of Accessibility: June to October

Predominant trail surface: Gravel, Rock, Dirt, Loose Rock

Hazards: Slick Rock, Bogs, Rock Slides, Steep Sections of Trail, Narrow Trail with Steep Drop-offs, Busy Road Crossings

Description of Hazards: There are very rocky sections of the trail.

Current Level Of Use:
(High - greater than 7 in group; Low - 3 or less.)

Horsemen: Low

Motorized: None

Bicyclists: Seldom

Hikers: Low

Tack & Equipment Dealers: Equus Equestrian Tack & Supply, 6400 N Business Loop Rd, PARK CITY, (435) 615–7433

Police: SUMMIT COUNTY SHERIFF, 6300 Silver Creek Drive, Park City, 84098, (435)615–3500

Veterinarian: Arcadia Veterinary Clinic, 90 E 1520 N Hwy 40, Heber, (435) 654–0592

Hospitals: Heber Valley Medical Center, 1485 South Highway 40, HEBER CITY, , (435) 654–2500

Gov Agency: Wasatch-Cache National Forest, 125 South State Street, Salt Lake City, 84138, (801) 236–3400

Other comments: The weather can change from hot to snow in the same day, go prepared for anything. This is a vast, roadless area; it is easy to get lost and turned around.

SMITH & MOREHOUSE TRAIL, FROM CRYSTAL LAKE

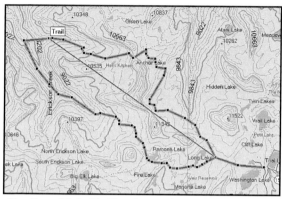

The Crystal Lake Trailhead opens the traveler to a variety of trails leading to many of the lakes in the Lakes Country.

Topo Map: Mirror Lake - #40110-F8-TF-024, Erickson Basin–40111-F1-TF-024

Name of Trailhead : Crystal Lake Trailhead

Name of Trail: Smith & Morehouse Trail

Trail #: 061

Property of: UNITED STATES FOREST SERVICE

Other Trails used by this route: Lakes Country Trail - #066

Connecting Trails: Middle Fork of the Weber - #076, North Fork Provo River - #075

Directions from the closest town to trailhead: Traveling east from Kamas on highway 150, go about 25 miles to the Trial Lake turn off. Turn north (left) at the sign and follow the road about one mile to the Crystal Lake Trailhead

Road Conditions: This road is paved all the way to the trailhead. Highway 150 is closed in the winter months.

Parking instructions: There is public parking for all types of users. Park anywhere.

Parking capacity: 15 Trucks and Trailers
Direction of trail from parking area: The trail is west of the trailhead.

Elevation at T/H: 10,000
Highest Elevation: 10,813
Steepest Grade: 17%
GPS T/H Longitude:110°45′ 56.45″W
GPS T/H Latitude: 40°40′ 59.05″N
Number of feet Climbing: 4,960

Camping and use restrictions at trailhead and along route: Water For Stock, Primitive Camping, Weed Free Hay, Camping at T/H, Dispersed Camping
Difficulty: Moderate
To complete this route, horses need to be: Moderately Fit.
Trail Route & Directions: Follow the Smith and Morehouse trail west from the Crystal Lake area. The trail passes Long Lake, Island Lake, Anchor Lake, and Adax Lake.
General description of route: The area is a forest/ alpine area with pine and Quaken Aspen trees. The trail is a single track trail, mostly dirt, passing marshy areas as well as some steep ledges. There are many scenic areas, including several lakes.
Type of Route: Loop
Length of Route in Miles: 17.7
Estimated travel time: 6 Hours
Route Attractions: Scenery, Fishing, Drinking Water and Campsites.
Other Attractions: The wildlife includes moose, black bear, elk, and mule deer.

Normal Temperatures during recommended months of use:
Spring: Cold to Cool
Summer: Mild
Fall: Cool to Cold
Months of Accessibility: June to October

Predominant trail surface: Gravel, Rock, Dirt, Loose Rock

Other surfaces: Slick Rock.

Hazards: Slick Rock, Deep or Wide Water Crossings, Bogs, Rock Slides and Steep Sections of Trail.

Description of Hazards: The boggy areas are covered with "corduroy" bridges.

Current Level Of Use:
(High - greater than 7 in group; Low - 3 or less.)
Horsemen: Low
Motorized: None
Bicyclists: None
Hikers: Moderate

Tack & Equipment Dealers: S Bar S Saddle Tack & Western Wear, 54 N Main St, KAMAS, 84036, (435) 783–4217

Police: SUMMIT COUNTY SHERIFF, 6300 Silver Creek Drive, Park City, 84098, (435)615–3500

Veterinarian: Isom Wade P D.V.M., 895 W 100 South, HEBER CITY, 84032, (435) 654–3837

Hospitals: Heber Valley Medical Center, 1485 South Highway 40, HEBER CITY,
(435) 654–2500

Gov Agency: Wasatch-Cache National Forest, 125 South State Street, Salt Lake City, 84138, (801) 236–3400

Other comments: Harsh weather changes any time of year. This is a vast primitive area. It is easy to get lost. Go prepared.

SO. JORDAN RIVER PARK, SALT LAKE COUNTY

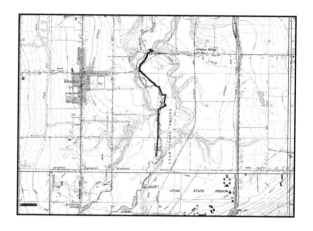

Topo Map: Midvale, USGF #40111-E8-TF-024
Name of Trailhead: 12300 S. 1000 West.
Name of Trail: So. Jordan River Park, Salt Lake County
Property of: South Jordan and Draper Cities.
Directions from the closest town to trailhead: Go to 12300 S. 1000 West.
Road Conditions: It is paved to trailhead.
Parking instructions: There is a public parking area used for hikers, bicyclists etc. Park anywhere.
Parking capacity: 15 Trucks and Trailers
Direction of trail from parking area: Travel west from the parking lot to the river and under the 12300 South bridge.

Elevation at T/H: 4,302
Highest Elevation: 4,371
Steepest Grade: 5%
GPS T/H Longitude: 111°55′ 4.53″W
GPS T/H Latitude: 40°31′ 37.10″N
Number of feet Climbing: 147

Camping and use restrictions at trailhead and along route: Water for Stock.

Other Restrictions: This area is high use for hikers, roller skaters, and bicyclists.

Difficulty: Easy **To complete this route, horses need to be:** Sound Only

Trail Route & Directions: From the trailhead, travel west and under the 12300 So. underpass. On the south side of the underpass, follow the road to the trail. The trail follows the paved trail on the east side. The trail ends at the Bangerter Highway.

General description of route: The route follows the river bottoms along the Jordan River. The area is wetlands with beautiful grass and reed areas. There is plenty of wildlife, such as mule deer, elk, ducks, geese, and blue herring.

Type of Route: Out and Back.

Length of Route in Miles: 4

Estimated travel time: 2 Hours.

Route Attractions: Scenery, Fishing, Conditioning, Drinking Water, Cell Phone Accessible and Restrooms.

Normal Temperatures during recommended months of use:

Winter: Cool to Cold

Spring: Cool to Mild

Summer: Hot

Fall: Cool to Mild

Months of Accessibility: Fall to Spring

Predominant trail surface: Sand, Gravel, Rock, Dirt, Loose Rock

Hazards: Deep or Wide Water Crossings, Narrow Bridges. Tunnel

Current Level of Use:
(High - greater than 7 in group; Low - 3 or less.)
Horsemen: Moderate
Motorized: Not Allowed
Bicyclists: Moderate
Hikers: Moderate

Tack & Equipment Dealers: Saddle Up, 11415 S Redwood Rd, SOUTH JORDAN, 84095 - 7804, (801) 254–5700

Police: Salt Lake County Sheriff, 2001 S State, Salt Lake City, 84190, (801) 468–3931

Veterinarian: South Valley Large Animal Clinic, 1791 W 11400 South, SOUTH JORDAN, 84095, (801) 254–2333

Hospitals: Alta View Hospital, 9660 S 1300 E, Sandy, 84094, 801) 501–2600

Gov Agency: Draper City Offices, 12441 S. 900 E., Draper, 84020, (801)576–6500

Other comments: Great for spring conditioning or winter riding. Look for lots of wildlife - deer, geese, ducks etc.

Looking northwest across the Jordan River from the trailhead.

SOUTH WILLOW, STANSBURY MOUNTAINS

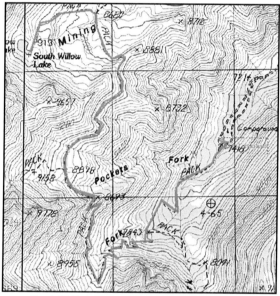

South Willow Lake from the Loop Campground.

Topo Map: Deseret Peak East, # 40112-D5-TF-024
Name of Trailhead: Loop Campground
Name of Trail: South Willow, Stansbury Mountains
Trail #: 036
Property of: UNITED STATES FOREST SERVICE
Connecting Trails: Front Trail - #031, Deseret Peak–#39
Directions from the closest town to trailhead: From
    Grantsville to the north of the Stansbury Mountains, it
    is 9.5 miles to the Loop Camp Ground. From highway
    40 (Main Street of Grantsville), turn south on Cooley's
    Lane. Look for the Forest Service sign. Follow the road
    south to the sign indicating South Willow Canyon,
    about 5.25 miles. Turn west on the dirt road and follow
    the road to the Loop Campground. The campground is
    about another 4.25 miles.

Road Conditions: Roads include I-80 to Grantsville, a two lane highway to and from Grantsville, and a dirt road to the Loop Campground. The dirt road is normally graded and passable; however, it is narrow near the Loop Campground and can be muddy and slippery when wet.

Parking instructions: Parking is along the road and in campsites. The parking lot is too small to park a truck and horse trailer.

Parking capacity: 7 Trucks and Trailers

Direction of trail from parking area: The trail leaves the campground from the west.

Elevation at T/H: 7,396
Highest Elevation: 9,155
Steepest Grade: 29%
GPS T/H Longitude: 112°36′ 21.24″W
GPS T/H Latitude: 40°28′ 59.26″N
Number of feet Climbing: 971

Camping and use restrictions at trailhead and along route: Water for Stock, Primitive Camping, Weed Free Hay, Camping at T/H, Dispersed Camping

Other Restrictions: The road to the campground is narrow and one-way at the end. Larger trucks and trailers may have trouble. Most of the trail is in a wilderness area and is restricted to wilderness uses.

Difficulty: Moderate

To complete this route, horses need to be: Moderately Fit

Trail Route & Directions: The route leaves the Loop Campground from the west end of the campground parking lot. Traveling west, the trail turns north and follows a steep canyon to the northeast and finally turns northwest to South Willow Lake.

General description of route: The trail is a popular trail and is generally well maintained by the Forest Service. The route is forest covered from the campground, heading west. The forest includes Douglas Fir, Mountain Mahogany, Quaken Aspen, Pinyon Pine, and Junipers. As the trail turns north, the trail is exposed on a south facing slope that is steep off of the south side. At the ridge, the trail turns west again through the trees and a grassy basin just below the South Willow Lake. There is a cross road of trails in the basin. Keep going generally west to continue on to the lake.

Type of Route: Out and Back.

Length of Route in Miles: 8.5

Estimated travel time: 4 Hours

Route Attractions: Scenery, Drinking Water and Campsites.

Other Attractions: Lots of wildlife and normally very few travelers are in the area. Especially abundant is the mule deer population. Much of the area is in the Deseret Peak Wilderness, which prohibits mechanical travel.

**Normal Temperatures during
recommended months of use:**
Spring: Cold
Summer: Cool to Hot
Fall: Cool
Months of Accessibility: Early June to late October

Predominant trail surface: Gravel, Rock, Dirt, Loose Rock

Hazards: Rock Slides, Steep Sections of Trail, Narrow Trail with Steep Drop-offs

Description of Hazards : The area where the trail is narrow with Steep Drop-offs is normally well maintained and is rarely impassable. The approach to South Willow Lake can be covered with deep snow as late as the early part of June.

Current Level Of Use:
(High - greater than 7 in group; Low - 3 or less.)
Horsemen: Low
Motorized: Not Allowed
Bicyclists: Not Allowed
Hikers: Low

Tack & Equipment Dealers: A. A. Callister Corp, 3615 S Redwood Rd, West Valley City, 84119, (801) 973–7058

Police: TOOELE SHERIFF, 47 S MAIN ST, TOOELE, (435) 665–2228

Veterinarian: Countryside Animal Clinic, 254 S Main St, TOOELE, (435) 882–4100

Hospitals: Mountain West Medical Center, 2055 N Main, TOOELE, (435) 843–3600

Gov Agency: Wasatch-Cache National Forest, 125 South State Street, Salt Lake City, 84138, (801) 236–3400

Other comments: The view from the top looks out over the Tooele City, the Oquirrh and Wasatch Mountains. The Great Salt Lake and parts of the Wasatch Front can also be seen.

The Great Salt Lake and Grantsville as seen from the South Willow Trail.

SOUTHEAST - BONNEVILLE SHORE LINE TRAIL

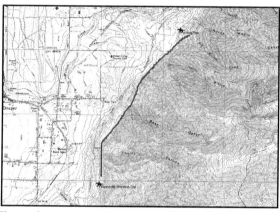

The southeast portion of the Bonneville Shoreline Trail can be accessed from Willow Park or the Corner Canyon Trial.

Topo Map: Draper, # 40111-E7-TF-024
Name of Trailhead: Corner Canyon Road, Draper
Name of Trail: Bonneville Shore Line Trail
Property of: UNITED STATES FOREST SERVICE
Connecting Trails: Cherry Canyon.
Directions from the closest town to trailhead: In Draper, go to 1300 East and 123000 South. Turn south and follow the roundabout east to Pioneer Road. Turn south on 2000 East and follow it to the dirt road. Follow the dirt road about one mile. The trail is on the east side of the road.
Road Conditions: The road is paved through Draper and graded dirt the final mile. Generally the roads are good to travel.
Parking instructions: Park along side the road. It is wide enough for traffic to pass.
Parking capacity: 10 Trucks and Trailers
Direction of trail from parking area: East side of the road.

Elevation at T/H: 5,150
Highest Elevation: 5,410
Steepest Grade: 27%
GPS T/H Longitude: 111°50′ 34.15″W
GPS T/H Latitude: 40°30′ 27.79″N
Number of feet Climbing: 966

Camping and use restrictions at trailhead and along route: Weed Free Hay
Difficulty: Moderate
To complete this route, horses need to be: Sound Only
Trail Route & Directions: Follow the trail northeast as it winds up the Bonneville Shore Line benches. Follow it north to Willow Park.
General description of route: The route starts out easy as it travels towards Bear Creek. At Bear Creek there is a narrow wooden bridge. At that point, the trail rises thru several steep switchbacks and through Oaks, Maples, Cedars and other brush.
Type of Route: Out and Back.
Length of Route in Miles: 6
Estimated travel time: 2 Hours
Route Attractions: Scenery and Conditioning.
Other Attractions: Much of the trail is exposed while some of it is shaded. The exposed areas offer great views of the Salt Lake Valley.

Normal Temperatures during recommended months of use:
Winter: Cold
Spring: Cold to Mild
Summer: Hot
Fall: Mild to Cold
Months of Accessibility: Year-round

Predominant trail surface: Sand, Gravel, Rock, Dirt, Loose Rock

Hazards: Narrow Bridges, Steep Sections of Trail

Description of Hazards: The switchbacks are not well planned and are a little tricky on the turns.

Current Level Of Use:
(High - greater than 7 in group; Low - 3 or less.)
Horsemen: Low
Motorized: Not Allowed
Bicyclists: Moderate
Hikers: Moderate

Tack & Equipment Dealers: Draper IFA Country Stores, 1071 E Pioneer Rd, Draper, 84020, (801) 571–0125

Police: Salt Lake County Sheriff, 2001 S State, Salt Lake City, 84190, (801) 468–3931

Veterinarian: South Valley Large Animal Clinic, 1791 W 11400 South, SOUTH JORDAN, 84095, (801) 254–2333

Hospitals: Alta View Hospital, 9660 S 1300 E, Sandy, 84094, (801) 501–2600

Gov Agency: Wasatch-Cache National Forest, 125 South State Street, Salt Lake City, 84138, (801) 236–3400

Other comments: There is one portion of the trail near Willow Park that may have a gate crossing the trail. The gate is there because of a dispute with a landowner and the local cities. You may need to turn around at that point.

*A dispersed trailhead along Corner Canyon Road,
just across from where the trail picks up.*

SPANISH VALLEY ROAD TO JOHNSON ON TOP

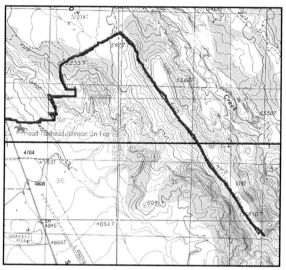

Johnson on Top offers wonderful views of the Moab area and surrounding red rock country.

Topo Map: Rill Creek, # 38109-E4-TF-024

Name of Trailhead: Spanish Valley Road

Name of Trail: Spanish Valley Road to Johnson on Top

Property of: BUREAU OF LAND MANAGEMENT

Directions from the closest town to trailhead: Follow Highway 191 south from Moab about 7.5 miles and turn east on the gravel pit road. Travel about 1/2 mile to Spanish Valley Road. Turn north and follow the road about one mile to the dirt road leaving the highway on the east side.

Road Conditions: Highway 191 and the Spanish Valley roads are paved and well maintained.

Parking instructions: Park along the Spanish Valley Road.

Parking capacity: 20 Trucks and Trailers

Direction of trail from parking area: East side of the road.

Elevation at T/H: 4,790
Highest Elevation: 5,790
Steepest Grade: 22%
GPS T/H Longitude: 109°27' 30.34"W
GPS T/H Latitude: 38°30' 8.93"N
Number of feet Climbing: 1,070

Camping and use restrictions at trailhead and along route: Weed Free Hay

Difficulty: Moderate

To complete this route, horses need to be: Moderately Fit

Trail Route & Directions: Follow the four wheel jeep track east/northeast from the highway about 2 miles to the trail traveling southeast and up the hill. Take the trail along the top of the plateau to the overlook of Kens Lake, on the southeast end.

General description of route: The route is a jeep trail in the open desert for the first two miles. The remainder of the route is a mixture of jeep trail and open country with other trails. The red rock terrain is vegetated with cedars, grasses, and brush.

Type of Route: Out and Back.

Length of Route in Miles: 8

Estimated travel time: 2.5 Hours

Route Attractions: Scenery, Conditioning and Cell Phone Accessible.

Other Attractions: Fabulous views of the valley and red rock country around the city of Moab.

Normal Temperatures during recommended months of use:
Winter: Cool to Cold
Spring: Cool to Mild
Summer: Hot
Fall: Hot to Cool
Months of Accessibility: Year round

Predominant trail surface: Jeep Trail, Dirt
Hazards: Steep Sections of Trail.

Current Level Of Use:
(High - greater than 7 in group; Low - 3 or less.)
Horsemen: Low
Motorized: Moderate
Bicyclists: Moderate
Hikers: Seldom

Tack & Equipment Dealers: Spanish Valley Feed Store, 2728 S Hwy 191, (435) 259 6315
Police: Grand County Sheriff, 125 E. Center, Moab, (435) 259–8115
Veterinarian: Moab Veterinary Clinic, 4575 Spanish Valley Dr, Moab, (435) 259–8710
Hospitals: Allen Memorial Hospital, 719 West Fourth Street, Moab, Tel.1–435–259–7191
Gov Agency: BUREAU OF LAND MANAGEMENT Field Office - Moab, 82 East Dogwood, Moab, 84532, (435) 259–2100
Other comments: The area is popular with bicyclists, ATVs, and four wheel vehicles–use caution. The area has very little water for stock.

STEEL HOLLOW

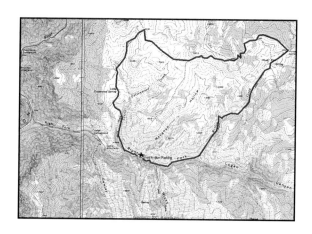

Topo Map: Temple Fork - #4111-G5-TF-024

Name of Trailhead (T/H): Little Cottonwood to Willow Creek

Name of Trail: Steel Hollow

Property of: USFS

Connecting Trails: Cowley Canyon, Rick's Canyon, Temple Fork, Willis Sink

Directions from the closest town to trailhead: From Logan, take highway 89 east about ten miles to mile marker 383. Turn right and proceed 1.8 miles along the right fork of the Logan River. At the Lomia Girls Camp, proceed east about .6 miles east along the north side of the river and past the stock corrals.

Road Conditions: It is a paved two lane highway to the turn off to the girls camp. Then it is dirt to the parking area.

Parking instructions: Park along the road.

Parking capacity: 5 Trucks and Trailers

Direction of trail from parking area: West

Elevation at T/H: 7,060
Highest Elevation: 6,910
Steepest Grade: 12%
GPS T/H Longitude: 111°36′ 6.41″W
GPS T/H Latitude: 41°46′ 21.20″N
Number of feet Climbing: 1,865

Camping and use restrictions at trailhead and along route: Water For Stock, Weed Free Hay, Camping at Trailhead

Difficulty: Moderate

To complete this route, horses need to be: Moderately Fit

Trail Route & Directions: Ride back to the stock corrals. Go behind the corrals and follow the trail north along the east side of Little Cottonwood Creek. The trail crosses the creek and up a steep, narrow section of trail as it climbs the west bank of the creek. At the top of the grade, the route passes a pond on the right. Follow the trail north through open country. Follow the jeep trail north to the fence. After passing through the gate, ride east. The trail passes another stock corral. Follow the trail to the right down the west bank of Willow Creek. Follow the creek to Steel Hollow. Keeping right, follow the trail east. Cross another creek just before the return to the parking lot.

General description of route: The trail is in a forested area. Crossing many creeks and the open areas can be boggy.

Type of Route: Loop

Length of Route in Miles: 10

Estimated travel time: 4 Hours

Route Attractions: Scenery, Campsite.

Other Attractions: Plenty of water for stock, stock corrals and campgrounds.

Normal Temperatures during recommended months of use:
Spring: Cold to Cool
Summer: Cool to Hot
Fall: Mild to Cold
Months of Accessibility: May to October

Predominant trail surface: Jeep Trail, Dirt
Hazards: Bogs, Steep Sections of Trail
Description of Hazards: One area is rocky, set and slippery.

Current Level of Use:
(High - greater than 7 in group; Low - 3 or less.)
Horsemen: Moderate
Motorized:
Seldom
Bicyclists: Moderate
Hikers: Low

Tack & Equipment Dealers: C-A-L Ranch Stores, 1224 N. Main St., Logan (435) 753–0611

Police: CACHE COUNTY SHERIFF, 50 West 200 North, Logan, 84321, (435)752–4103

Veterinarian: Cache Meadow Veterinary Clinic, 38 E. 2600 N. Logan, (435) 725–6135

Hospitals: Logan Regional Hospital, 1400 N. 500 E., Logan, (435) 716–4000

Gov Agency: Wasatch-Cache National Forest, 125 South State Street, Salt Lake City, 84138, (801) 236–3400

STEELE BENCH ROAD TO THE HENRY'S MOUNTAINS

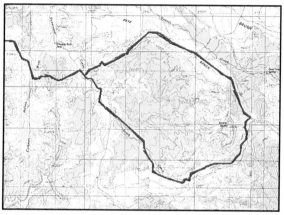

There are very few trails on the north west side of the Henry Mountains. This route follows a jeep track.

Topo Map: Steele Butte, #38110-A8-TF-024

Name of Trailhead: Sandy Ranch

Name of Trail: Steele Bench Road to the Henry's Mountains

Property of: BUREAU OF LAND MANAGEMENT

Other Trails used by this route: South Creek Road.

Directions from the closest town to trailhead: Turn south on the Notum Road, which is 20 miles east of Torrey. Follow the road 10.3 miles to the jeep road leaving east from Notum Road. Follow the dirt road 6 miles to the Sandy Ranch. Drive past the ranch about 2 miles and find a place to park along the road. There are a lot of side dirt roads and it is easy to get off on the wrong road. Stay on the left fork when coming on the first three splits, and take right fork on the fourth split.

Road Conditions: The road from Torrey is a two lane paved highway to Notum Road. Notum Road is a graded dirt road but can be difficult to travel when wet. The dirt road leaving the Notum road is rough and should not be traveled when wet.

Parking instructions: Park along side the road.

Parking capacity: 20 Trucks and Trailers

Direction of trail from parking area: The road is the trail, follow it.

Elevation at T/H: 5,670
Highest Elevation: 6,200
Steepest Grade: 17%
GPS T/H Longitude: 110°58′ 2.37″W
GPS T/H Latitude: 38°5′ 14.77″N
Number of feet Climbing: 684

Camping and use restrictions at trailhead and along route: Weed Free Hay, Camping at T/H, Dispersed Camping

Other Restrictions: There is very little water. Take your own supply for the stock and yourself. There is water at the line camp at the Sandy Ranch.

Difficulty: Moderate

To complete this route, horses need to be: Moderately Fit

Trail Route & Directions: Follow the road out from either the left or right. The road is easy to follow and is passable by four wheel vehicles and ATVs.

General description of route: The route is a road lined by trees and clear cut areas. The clear cut areas were established to provide forage for the bison herd.

Type of Route: Loop

Length of Route in Miles: 14

Estimated travel time: 5 Hours

Route Attractions: Scenery, Conditioning and Campsites.

Other Attractions: There is a campground at a spring on the northeast part of the trail.

Normal Temperatures during recommended months of use:
Winter: Cold
Spring: Cold to Cool
Summer: Mild to Hot
Fall: Cool to Cold
Months of Accessibility: October to May

Predominant trail surface: Sand, Gravel, Rock, Jeep Trail, Dirt, Loose Rock

Hazards: Steep Sections of Trail

Description of Hazards: The jeep trail does have some ATV traffic. This is an area with a large bison herd. Travel with caution. Bison can outrun saddle stock on a short sprint.

Current Level of Use:
(High - greater than 7 in group; Low - 3 or less.)
Horsemen: Low
Motorized: Low
Bicyclists: Low
Hikers: None

Tack & Equipment Dealers: Loa Builders Supply, 137 N. Main, Loa, (435)836–2751

Police: WAYNE COUNTY SHERIFF, Wayne County Courthouse, Loa, 84747, (435)836–2789

Veterinarian: Tri County Veterinary Hospital, 352 E. 200 N. Torrey, (435)425–3487

Hospitals: Castle View Hospital, 300 N. Hospital Dr., Price, 84501, (435) 637–4800

Gov Agency: BUREAU OF LAND MANAGEMENT Field Office - Richfield, 150 East 900 North, Richfield, 84701, (435) 896–1500

Other comments: There are some trails made by the Bison;

however, they are hard to follow.

*The Henry Mountains in the background supports a bison
herd that migrates to the Mountains every spring.*

STILLWATER FORK TO AMETHYST LAKE

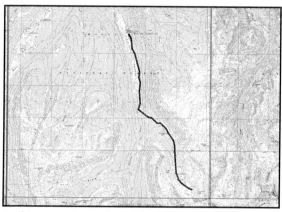

The trail is easy going to the Ostler Fork trail, and very picturesque.
The Ostler Fork portion starts out steep and up some slick rock.

Topo Map: Christmas Meadow, # 40110-G7-TF-0224
Name of Trailhead: Christmas Meadows
Name of Trail: Stillwater Fork to Amethyst Lake
Trail #: 098
Property of: UNITED STATES FOREST SERVICE
Other Trails used by this route: Ostler Fork - #149
Connecting Trails: West Basin - #139, Main Fork–#097, Smiths Fork -#091
Directions from the closest town to trailhead: On highway 150 south of Evanston, Wyoming, travel to the Utah border. From the border, travel about 9 miles to the road turning east/southeast. (The road is about a mile south of the Bear River Ranger Station.) Follow the road about 4 miles southeast to the trailhead and campground.
Road Conditions: Highway 150 is well maintained, but closed during the winter. The dirt road is a well maintained and used for the summer cabins in the area.

Parking instructions: The trailhead is past the campgrounds. It was not well developed for equestrians, but there is plenty of parking along the perimeter.

Parking capacity: 15 Trucks and Trailers

Direction of trail from parking area: This trail starts just southeast of the restrooms.

Elevation at T/H: 8,800
Highest Elevation: 10,765
Steepest Grade: 17%
GPS T/H Longitude: 110°48′ 3.09″W
GPS T/H Latitude: 40°49′ 25.93″N
Number of feet Climbing: 2,340

Camping and use restrictions at trailhead and along route: Water For Stock, Potable Water, Weed Free Hay, Camping at T/H, Dispersed Camping

Other Restrictions: Amethyst Lake is in the High Uintas wilderness area. Wilderness restrictions apply.

Difficulty: Moderate

To complete this route, horses need to be: Moderately Fit

Trail Route & Directions: From the trailhead, travel 2.5 miles south to the Ostler Fork Trail. Turn on that trail southeast as it climbs up the mountain. Amethyst Lake is about another 4 miles.

General description of route: This route starts out following an alpine area through pine trees and meadows. This portion of the trail rises very little. There are many boggy areas that are covered with bridging materials. The Ostler Fork Trail, unlike the Christmas Meadows Trail, starts out going up hill very rapidly. The uphill portion does contain some slick rock areas that are not too difficult. The remainder of the trail is over the hill and down the drainage to the lake.

Type of Route: Out and Back.

Length of Route in Miles: 13
Estimated travel time: 4.5 Hours
Route Attractions: Scenery, Fishing, Conditioning, Drinking Water, RV Facilities. , Campsites and Restrooms.
Other Attractions: There are small fish in the many streams and lakes in the area. This drainage has a large moose population. It is possible to see 10 to 15 moose in a day. The emerald green Amethyst Lake provides great fishing for pan-size cutthroat and brook trout.

Normal Temperatures during recommended months of use:
Spring: Cold to Warm
Summer: Cool to Warm
Fall: Cool to Cold
Months of Accessibility: June to early October

Predominant trail surface: Sand, Gravel, Rock, Jeep Trail, Dirt, Loose Rock
Other surfaces: Wood bridges over the bogs.
Hazards: Slick Rock, Bogs, Narrow Bridges, Steep Sections of Trail
Description of Hazards: The narrow bridges do not have hand rails or anything to impede horse travel.

Current Level of Use:
(High - greater than 7 in group; Low - 3 or less.)
Horsemen: Moderate
Motorized: Not Allowed
Bicyclists: None
Hikers: Moderate

Tack & Equipment Dealers: Lazy Sb Leather & Saddlery, FT BRIDGER, WY 82933, (307) 782–7300
Police: MOUNTAIN VIEW SHERIFF, 77 COUNTY ROAD

109, EVANSTON, WY, (307) 782–3682

Veterinarian: Bear River Veterinary Clinic, 619 Almy Road #107, N OF EVANSTON, WY, (307) 789–5230

Hospitals: Evanston Regional Hospital, 190 Arrowhead Dr, Evanston, WY 82930 - 9266, (307) 789–3636

Gov Agency: Wasatch-Cache National Forest, 125 South State Street, Salt Lake City, 84138, (801) 236–3400

Other comments: This area contains many cabins and has quite a bit of foot traffic around Christmas Meadows. Camping and horse feed around Amethyst Lake is poor. Camp at the lower meadows.

STRAWBERRY NARROWS TRAIL, STRAWBERRY RESERVOIR

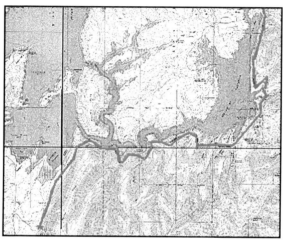

*Take your fishing Pole! There is plenty of
opportunity to fish along the lake.*

Topo Map: Strawberry Res. SE, # 40111-A1-TF-024

Name of Trailhead: Narrows West Trailhead

Name of Trail: Strawberry Narrows Trail, Strawberry Reservoir

Trail #: 304

Property of: UNITED STATES FOREST SERVICE

Directions from the closest town to trailhead: From Heber City, travel east on State Highway 40 towards Strawberry Reservoir. Turn south on highway to the Strawberry Visitors Center and follow the road past the reservoir about 17 miles. Turn north at Renegade Point to the Narrows West Trailhead, or go past the trailhead and turn east on the dirt road and travel about 1 mile to a dispersed trailhead.

Road Conditions: All of the roads are well maintained except the dirt road. If the dirt road is impassable, parking on or near the highway is acceptable.

Parking instructions: Parking in near the Renegade Point boat ramp.

Parking capacity: 10 Trucks and Trailers

Direction of trail from parking area: By traveling north along the southeast part of the reservoir, it is easy to pick up the trail.

Elevation at T/H: 7,967
Highest Elevation: 7,967
Steepest Grade: 10%
GPS T/H Longitude: 111°08' 51.52"W
GPS T/H Latitude: 40°07' 13.26"N
Number of feet Climbing: 292

Camping and use restrictions at trailhead and along route: Water For Stock, Potable Water, Weed Free Hay, Camping at T/H, Dispersed Camping

Difficulty: Easy

To complete this route, horses need to be: Sound Only

Trail Route & Directions: Travel north along the southeast portion of Strawberry Reservoir and follow the route east along the edge of the reservoir. The trail ends at the Aspen Grove parking lot.

General description of route: The route starts out in the sagebrush below Poison Ridge and travels in the trees along the narrows to Aspen Grove. The trail does very little climbing, and there very little elevation change.

Type of Route: Out and Back.

Length of Route in Miles: 22

Estimated travel time: 7 Hours

Route Attractions: Scenery, Fishing, Conditioning, Drinking Water, RV Facilities, Campsites, Cell Phone Accessible and Restrooms.

Other Attractions: Great scenery with plenty of opportunities to fish.

**Normal Temperatures during
recommended months of use:**
Spring: Cold to Warm
Summer: Warm to Hot
Fall: Mild to Cold
Months of Accessibility: Mid May to October

Predominant trail surface: Jeep Trail, Dirt

Description of Hazards: The trail crosses a stream close to the lake, which can scare a horse that has not been around any lakes.

Current Level of Use:
(High - greater than 7 in group; Low - 3 or less.)
Horsemen: Moderate
Motorized: None
Bicyclists: Moderate
Hikers: Low

Tack & Equipment Dealers: Equus Equestrian Tack & Supply, 6400 N Business Loop Rd, PARK CITY, , (435) 615–7433

Police: SUMMIT COUNTY SHERIFF, 6300 Silver Creek Drive, Park City, 84098, (435)615–3500

Veterinarian: Arcadia Veterinary Clinic, 90 E 1520 N Hwy 40, Heber, (435) 654–0592

Hospitals: Heber Valley Medical Center, 1485 South Highway 40, HEBER CITY, , (435) 654–2500

Gov Agency: Wasatch-Cache National Forest, 125 South State Street, Salt Lake City, 84138, (801) 236–3400

Other comments: Be prepared–the weather can change rapidly in this area. It is almost always windy and/or rainy sometime during the day.

TIMPOONEKE TRAIL, AMERICAN FORK CANYON

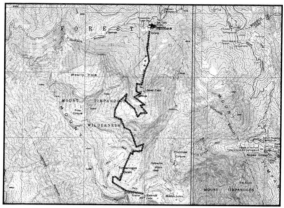

*The route climbs the "Giant Staircase" series of cliffs and rock-slides.
This is a wonderful area, the scenery and vista's cannot be equaled anywhere.
The map shows the route from Timpooneke to Emerald Lake on the southeast.*

Topo Map: Timpanogas Cave, # 40111-D5-TF-024
Name of Trailhead: Timpooneke Campground
Name of Trail: Timpooneke Trail, American Fork Canyon
Trail #: '053
Property of: UNITED STATES FOREST SERVICE
Other Trails used by this route: Timpanogas Trail - #052
Connecting Trails: Timpanogas Summit Trail - #054,
    Stewarts Cascade Trail - #055
Directions from the closest town to trailhead: From Alpine
    & Highland, travel east on Highway 92 to American
    Fork Canyon. Travel 8.25 miles from the mouth of the
    canyon to near the summit of the canyon. Just past the
    Altamont Campground, turn right at the Timpooneke
    Campground. Travel to the south through the camp-
    ground to the parking lots.
Road Conditions: Highway 92 is narrow but well main-
    tained. Use caution when passing the Timpanogas

National Park. It is 20 miles per hour in park.

Parking instructions: The parking lot can be very crowded on the weekends, especially in the fall months. There are two parking lots and some parking along the road.

Parking capacity: 20 Trucks and Trailers

Direction of trail from parking area: The trail is southwest of the parking lot. Follow the trail nearest the trail kiosk, about 25 yards from the parking lot.

Elevation at T/H: 7,382
Highest Elevation: 10,711
Steepest Grade: 24%
GPS T/H Longitude: 111°38′ 16.16″W
GPS T/H Latitude: 40°25′ 52.24″N
Number of feet Climbing: 4,315

Camping and use restrictions at trailhead and along route: Water For Stock, Potable Water, Primitive Camping, Weed Free Hay, Camping at T/H, Dispersed Camping. An equestrian campground is about 1/4 mile from the parking lots. The campground has livestock corrals and restrooms. There is a shelter at Emerald Lake, complete with a fireplace. It is large enough to sleep ten people.

Difficulty: Difficult

To complete this route, horses need to be: Moderately Fit

Trail Route & Directions: The trail leaves south and west of the parking lot. The route follows a well established trail, traveling generally south and south east.

General description of route: The route is steep going most of the way and rises about 4,000 feet in five miles. The route is somewhat rocky and crosses rock slides, creeks, and bogs. The bogs are covered with wood bridges. Most of the trail has Steep Drop-offs.

Type of Route: Out and Back.

Length of Route in Miles: 12 Miles
Estimated travel time: 6 Hours
Route Attractions: Scenery, Drinking Water, RV Facilities, Campsites and Restrooms.
Other Attractions: The Timpanogas Wilderness area is home to mountain goats, big horn sheep, moose, mule deer, elk, and other wildlife.

Normal Temperatures during recommended months of use:
Spring: Cool to Mild
Summer: Mild to Hot
Fall: Mild to Cold
Months of Accessibility: Late April to late October

Predominant trail surface: Rock, Dirt, Loose Rock
Other surfaces: Snow can be present at the higher elevations year-round.
Hazards: Bogs, Narrow Bridges, Rock Slides, Steep Sections of Trail, Narrow Trail with Steep Drop-offs
Description of Hazards: The last part of the trail out of the Timpanogas basin to Emerald Lake is narrow, steep, and crosses a rock slide for about 1/4 mile.

Current Level of Use:
(High - greater than 7 in group; Low - 3 or less.)
Horsemen: Low
Motorized: Not Allowed
Bicyclists: Not Allowed
Hikers: High

Tack & Equipment Dealers: Highland IFA Country Stores, 521 W 200 North, HIGHLAND, 84003 (801) 756–9604
Police: Utah County Sheriff, 84660, (801)851–4000

Veterinarian: Animal Clinic, 14255 S. State St. Orem, (801) 225–0774

Hospitals: Utah Valley Regional MED Center, 1034 N 500 W, Provo, 84604, (801) 357–7056

Gov Agency: Uinta National Forest, 88 West 100 North, Provo, 84601, (801) 342–5100

Other comments: Weather conditions change quickly. Be prepared for sun, wind, cold and hot weather. This route is not for first time riders or inexperienced horses. Horses should be in good condition, and there are some areas that may need to hiked.

This picture of the mountain goat was taken at Emerald Lake. We saw about 30 goats that day.

UNION PACIFIC RAIL TRAIL STATE PARK

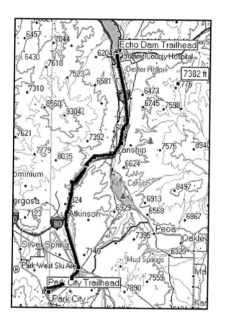

Topo Map: Coalville - #40111-H4-TF-024, Wanship–# 40111-G4-tf-024, Park City East -#40111-F$-TF-024, Park City West - #40111-F5-TF-024

Name of Trailhead: Echo Reservoir

Name of Trail: Union Pacific Rail Trail State Park

Property of: Union Pacific Rail Trail State Park

Directions from the closest town to trailhead: There is access from Coalville, Echo Reservoir, Wanship, or Park City. Echo Trailheads: the trail is accessible from the road from several areas along the reservoir. From the south, exit into Coalville. Turn left on the Main St. and head 7 miles north. Park City Trailhead: in Park City, take Kearns Boulevard to Bonanza Dr, then turn on Prospector Ave. to behind the Park City Plaza.

Road Conditions: Paved on either local or interstate roads.
Parking instructions: Echo Reservoir, park along the road.
Parking capacity: 5 Trucks and Trailers
Direction of trail from parking area: South along the rail
road tracks.

Elevation at T/H: 5,570
Highest Elevation: 6,860
Steepest Grade: 5%
GPS T/H Longitude: 111°24′ 55.60″W
GPS T/H Latitude: 40°55′ 38.55″N
Number of feet Climbing: 1,500

Difficulty: Easy
To complete this route, horses need to be: Sound Only
Trail Route & Directions: From Echo Reservoir, follow the
trail to Coalville, Wanship, and Park City.
General description of route: The terrain is diverse and
changes between Juniper, sage, rocks, Gambels Oak,
reservoirs, rivers, and farm land. The trail crosses the
interstate and through several small towns.
Type of Route: Out and Back.
Length of Route in Miles: 60
Estimated travel time: 20 Hours
Route Attractions: Scenery, Conditioning and Cell Phone
Accessible.
Other Attractions: Lots of scenery, great vistas. Fishing is
great along the Weber River.

**Normal Temperatures during
recommended months of use:**
Winter: Cold
Spring: Cold to Cool
Summer: Mild to High
Fall: Mild to Cold

Months of Accessibility: Year round, can
be icy and snowy in the winter.

Predominant trail surface: Gravel, Rock, Jeep Trail, Dirt
Other surfaces: Cinder and other materials used by the rail-
road.
Description of Hazards: The trail is a gentle grade that fol-
lows the Union Pacific train tracks and the freeway.
The trail along the tracks is cinder and dirt.

Current Level of Use:
(High - greater than 7 in group; Low - 3 or less.)
Horsemen: Low
Motorized: Not Allowed
Bicyclists: Moderate
Hikers: Low

Tack & Equipment Dealers: Equus Equestrian Tack &
Supply, 6400 N Business Loop Rd, PARK CITY,
(435) 615–7433
Police: SUMMIT COUNTY SHERIFF, 6300 Silver Creek
Drive, Park City, 84098, (435)615–3500
Veterinarian: White Pine Veterinary Clinic, 2100 Rasmussen
Rd. Park City, (435) 649–7182
Hospitals: Heber Valley Medical Center, 1485 South
Highway 40, HEBER CITY, (435) 654–2500
Gov Agency: Historic Union Pacific Rail Trail State Park,
P.O. Box 754, Park City, 84060–0754, (435–649–
6839)

WEST FORK - BLACKS FORK
TO DEAD HORSE LAKE

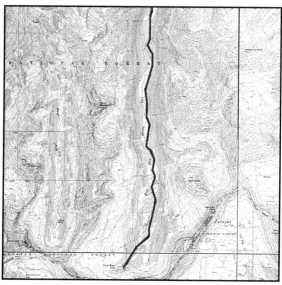

The trail to Dead Horse Lake and Dead Horse Pass, follows a southerly route about 10.5 miles one way. The highline trail passes the lake from Dead Horse Pass to Red Knob Pass.

Topo Map: Red Knob - # 40110-G6-TF-024

Name of Trailhead: West Fork - Blacks Fork

Name of Trail: West Fork - Blacks Fork to Dead Horse Lake

Trail #: 101

Property of: UNITED STATES FOREST SERVICE

Connecting Trails: Smiths Fork Trail - #091, East Fork - #102

Directions from the closest town to trailhead: On highway 150 south of Evanston, Wyoming, travel to the Utah border. From the border, travel about 6 miles to the road turning east. (The road is about a quarter mile north of the East Fork Campground.) Travel about 16

miles on the logging road to the smaller dirt road, turning south and following southwest. (The Lyman Lake turn-off is past the road south.) Take the road about 4.5 miles to the trailhead. There is not a formal trailhead. Park anywhere on either side of the river.

Road Conditions: Highway 150 is maintained throughout the spring to fall and closed for the winter. The dirt roads are usually graded and passable during the season; however, it maybe very washboardy.

Parking instructions: There is not a maintained parking lot. Park in any of the meadow areas north of the river, or the wooded area southwest of the river.

Parking capacity: 20 Trucks and Trailers

Direction of trail from parking area: Follow the jeep road across the river south/south west. Continue down the road about a mile to the trail. The trail follows an old road into the wilderness area.

Elevation at T/H: 9,300
Highest Elevation: 10,895
Steepest Grade: 5%
GPS T/H Longitude: 110°40′ 14.64″W
GPS T/H Latitude: 040°53′ 5.84″N
Number of feet Climbing: 2,280

Camping and use restrictions at trailhead and along route: Water For Stock , Primitive Camping, Weed Free Hay, Camping at T/H, Dispersed Camping

Other Restrictions: Dead Horse Lake is in the High Uintas Wilderness area. Wilderness restrictions apply.

Difficulty: Easy

To complete this route, horses need to be: Sound Only

Trail Route & Directions: Follow the trail south along the old road. There are a few gated fences to go through.

General description of route: The trail is in an alpine setting from start to finish, with many stream crossings. The route includes a forest of Douglas Fir, Mountain Mahogany, Scrub Oak, sagebrush flats, and many grassy meadows. The route is a gentle rise to the south, which should be easy for any sound horse.

Type of Route: Out and Back.

Length of Route in Miles: 15

Estimated travel time: 5.5 Hours

Route Attractions: Scenery, Fishing, Conditioning, Drinking Water and Campsites.

Other Attractions: The area has a lot of wildlife. The moose, mule deer, black bear, lynx, river otters, wolverine and elk are plentiful. The lake contains cutthroat trout.

Normal Temperatures during recommended months of use:
Summer: Cool to Warm
Fall: Warm to Cold
Months of Accessibility: June to early October

Predominant trail surface: Gravel, Rock, Jeep Trail, Dirt, Loose Rock

Other surfaces: This is an alpine area with many boggy meadows and streams.

Hazards: Bogs.

Current Level of Use:
(High - greater than 7 in group; Low - 3 or less.)
Horsemen: Low
Motorized: Not Allowed
Bicyclists: Not Allowed
Hikers: Low

Tack & Equipment Dealers: Lazy Sb Leather & Saddlery, FT BRIDGER, WY 82933, (307) 782–7300

Police: MOUNTAIN VIEW SHERIFF, 77 COUNTY ROAD 109, EVANSTON, WY, (307) 782–3682

Veterinarian: Bear River Veterinary Clinic, 619 Almy Road #107, N OF EVANSTON, WY, (307) 789–5230

Hospitals: Evanston Regional Hospital, 190 Arrowhead Dr, Evanston, WY 82930 - 9266, (307) 789–3636

Gov Agency: Wasatch-Cache National Forest, 125 South State Street, Salt Lake City, 84138, (801) 236–3400

Other comments: Horse feed for overnight camping may be scarce during the later part of the year. This area is grazed by sheep. Check with the Forest Service for feed conditions. Feed is usually available in the large meadows northeast of the lake.

Looking towards Red Knob Pass in a meadow east of Dead Horse Lake. The natural emerald green Dead Horse Lake is at the foot of Dead Horse pass above the rocky timberline.

WILDLIFE REFUGE UNIT NUMBER 4 AT CROYDEN

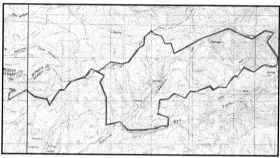

This wildlife habitat area is wide open to cross country travel, either by following the many roads or some limited trails.

Topo Map: Devils Slide, #41111-A5-TF-024

Name of Trailhead: Wildlife Refuge

Name of Trail: Wildlife Refuge Unit Number 4 at Croyden

Property of: Utah State Land

Directions from the closest town to trailhead: East of Morgan on I-84, take the exit to Croyden. It is the third exit east of Morgan. Follow the road northeast about 1.25 miles past the cement plant and keep right (east) at the fork in the road. When approaching Croyden, turn at the first right (southwest). About 1.8 miles from the interstate, just past the cemetery, turn east on to the dirt road, about 2.5 miles from the trailhead. Follow the road east to the trailhead. The trailhead has several hay mangers and tie rails just outside the fenced off wildlife preserve.

Road Conditions: The road leaving the interstate is a paved two lane highway. The dirt road to the trailhead is graded and usually well maintained.

Parking instructions: There is plenty of parking at the trailhead. Park anywhere in the area near the fence.

Parking capacity: 20 Trucks and Trailers

Direction of trail from parking area: The route leaves the parking lot through the gate on the east end of the parking area.

Elevation at T/H: 5,590
Highest Elevation: 7,621
Steepest Grade: 18%
GPS T/H Longitude: 111°30′ 48.10″W
GPS T/H Latitude: 041°03′ 32.53″N
Number of feet Climbing: 425

Camping and use restrictions at trailhead and along route: Water For Stock, Camping at T/H

Difficulty: Moderate

To complete this route, horses need to be: Sound Only

Trail Route & Directions: The area does not have a lot of trails. It is easier to follow the numerous jeep tracks. Follow the dirt road generally northeast. About five miles out, there is a spring in a wooded area. The route can follow any of the roads in the area and still have a great ride.

General description of route: The route starts out in the sagebrush covered foot hills and gains altitude as it winds northeast. Since there is not a specific trail or route, it is difficult to describe a route. The surrounding foliage includes sagebrush, cottonwoods, junipers and mountain mahogany.

Type of Route: Loop

Length of Route in Miles: 12.6

Estimated travel time: 4 Hours

Route Attractions: Scenery, Campsites, Cell Phone Accessible, Restrooms and Provisions for horses.

Other Attractions: Deer and elk winter in this area, and many can be seen in the early spring or late fall.

Normal Temperatures during recommended months of use:
Spring: Cold to Cool
Summer: Cool to Hot
Fall: Mild to Cold
Months of Accessibility: May to October

Predominant trail surface: Jeep Trail, Dirt
Hazards: Steep Sections of Trail
Description of Hazards: There are some steep areas along the dirt roads, but nothing very tough for most conditioned horses.

Current Level of Use:
(High - greater than 7 in group; Low - 3 or less.)
Horsemen: Moderate
Motorized: Low
Bicyclists: Seldom
Hikers: Seldom

Tack & Equipment Dealers: Dee's Tire & Farm Supply, 1845 S. Morgan Valley Dr., 84050, 801–829–6523
Police: Morgan County's Sheriff Office. 48 W Young St. Morgan, 84050. 911 or 801 829 0590.
Veterinarian: River Valley Vet Hospital, 395 N 400 E, Morgan, (801) 829–3632
Hospitals: MaKay-Dee Hospital, 4401 Harrison Boulevard, Ogden, 84403, 801–627–2800
Gov Agency: Utah Division of Wildlife Resources, 1594 W. North Temple, Salt Lake City, 84114, (801) 538–4700

YELLOW FORK TRAIL, SALT LAKE COUNTY

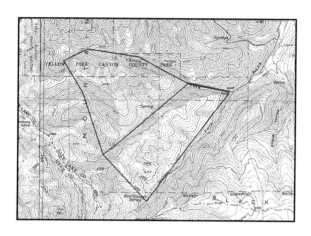

Topo Map: Tickville Spring, # 40112-D1-TF-024
Name of Trailhead (T/H): Yellow Fork Trailhead
Name of Trail: Yellow Fork Trail, Salt Lake County
Property of: Salt Lake County
Directions from the closest town to trailhead: Take Highway 71 to Herriman. From the fire station on Main Street in Herriman, travel 1/2 mile west to the Rose Canyon Road. Turn south, travel one mile, and turn west. Follow the road four and one half miles to the Yellow Fork trailhead.
Road Conditions: The paved two-lane road is public to Rose Canyon. The dirt road at the end of the Rose Canyon road is private, and not well maintained. The road approaching the area is well maintained and passable year round.
Parking instructions: At the trailhead, parking is over the bridge to the south of the road.
Parking capacity: 15 Trucks and Trailers
Direction of trail from parking area: The trail is on the

north side of the bridge and leaves the area west of the parking area.

Elevation at T/H: 5,670
Highest Elevation: 7,565
Steepest Grade: 23%
GPS T/H Longitude: 112°05′ 1.33″W
GPS T/H Latitude: 40°27′ 55.56″N
Number of feet Climbing: 2,658

Camping and use restrictions at trailhead and along route: Water For Stock

Other Restrictions: Do not park in front of the home on the north side of the Yellow Fork Stream or along the side of the road east of the house.

Difficulty: Moderate

To complete this route, horses need to be: Sound Only

Trail Route & Directions: Follow the trail on the south side of the stream and road. Keeping south of the picnic area, travel west up the canyon. The trail crosses over a saddle to the north and comes back down the canyon past the picnic area. Follow the trail west of the picnic area and back to the trail leading into the park.

General description of route: The route is scrub-oak and maple covered most of the route. Most of the route is easy going with very few steep areas. This is a great trail for early riding season conditioning.

Type of Route: Loop

Length of Route in Miles 7

Estimated travel time: 3 Hours

Route Attractions: Scenery, Campsites, Cell Phone Accessible Restrooms.

Normal Temperatures during recommended months of use:
Spring: Cold to Mild
Summer: Mild to Hot
Fall: Mild to Cool
Months of Accessibility: April to November

Predominant trail surface: Jeep Trail, Dirt

Current Level of Use:
(High - greater than 7 in group; Low - 3 or less.)
Horsemen: Moderate
Motorized: Seldom
Bicyclists: Low
Hikers: Low

Tack & Equipment Dealers: Saddle Up, 11415 S Redwood Rd, SOUTH JORDAN, 84095 - 7804, (801) 254–5700

Police: Salt Lake County Sheriff, 2001 S State, Salt Lake City, 84190, (801) 468–3931

Veterinarian: South Valley Large Animal Clinic, 1791 W 11400 South, SOUTH JORDAN, 84095, (801) 254–2333

Hospitals: Jordan Valley Hospital, 3580 W. 9000 S., West Jordan, (801) 561–8888

Gov Agency: Salt Lake County Parks and Rec. Adm., 2001 South State Street S4400, Salt Lake City, 84190, (801)483–5473

Other comments: Great conditioning trail with easy access.

YELLOW PINE, UINTA MOUNTAINS

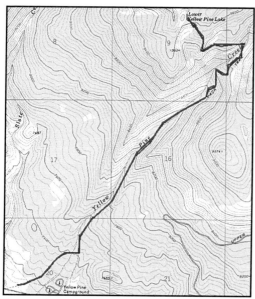

There is plenty of parking west of the campground area.
The trail follows the Yellow Pine Creek most of the way.

Topo Map: Hoyt Peak - # 40111-F2-TF-024
Name of Trailhead: Yellow Pine Campground
Name of Trail: Yellow Pine, Uinta Mountains
Trail #: 165
Property of: UNITED STATES FOREST SERVICE
Connecting Trails: Box Canyon Trail.
Directions from the closest town to trailhead: Taking Highway 150 about 6.3 miles, turn north on the dirt road. Park anywhere.
Road Conditions: Paved all the way. Closed in the winter.
Parking instructions: Park anywhere.
Parking capacity: 20 Trucks and Trailers
Direction of trail from parking area: The trail is east through the campground area.

Elevation at T/H: 7,100
Highest Elevation: 9,633
Steepest Grade: 20%
GPS T/H Longitude: 111°10' 39.02"W
GPS T/H Latitude: 040°37' 54.53"N
Number of feet Climbing: 2,566

Camping and use restrictions at trailhead and along route: Weed Free Hay, Camping at T/H, Dispersed Camping.

Difficulty: Moderate

To complete this route, horses need to be: Moderately Fit

Trail Route & Directions: Follow the trail northeast about 3 miles and turn north/northwest to the twin Yellow Pine Lakes

General description of route: The trail is generally tree covered most of the route and follows the Yellow Pine Creek most of the way. There are several stream crossings along the way with wood bridges.

Type of Route: Out and Back.

Length of Route in Miles: 7

Estimated travel time: 3.5 Hours

Route Attractions: Scenery, Fishing, Conditioning and Campsites.

Other Attractions: This area is home to a few moose and elk. Fishing in the two lakes is slow, and the fish are small.

Normal Temperatures during recommended months of use:
Summer: Cool to Mild
Fall: Cool to Cold
Months of Accessibility: June to October

Predominant trail surface: Rock, Dirt, Loose Rock
Other surfaces: Bridges cross the streams. The streams can be crossed without the bridges.

Hazards: Steep Sections of Trail.

Current Level of Use:
(High - greater than 7 in group; Low - 3 or less.)
Horsemen: Low
Motorized: None
Bicyclists: Seldom
Hikers: Low

Tack & Equipment Dealers: S Bar S Saddle Tack & Western Wear, 54 N Main St, KAMAS, 84036, (435) 783–4217

Police: SUMMIT COUNTY SHERIFF, 6300 Silver Creek Drive, Park City, 84098, (435)615–3500

Veterinarian: Isom Wade P D.V.M., 895 W 100 South, HEBER CITY, 84032, (435) 654–3837

Hospitals: Heber Valley Medical Center, 1485 South Highway 40, HEBER CITY, , (435) 654–2500

Gov Agency: Wasatch-Cache National Forest, 125 South State Street, Salt Lake City, 84138, (801) 236–3400

Other comments: Camping areas are limited around the lake, but there are several camping areas just before the lake. The view from the lake is spectacular. In the distance, Mount Timpanogas can be viewed.

Yellow Pine Lake at the top of the trail. The view includes the mountains around Kamas and on a clear day Mount Timpanogas can be seen in the distance.

55 OTHER TRAILS TO EXPLORE

Left Fork Tusher Canyon Book Cliffs	Book Cliffs
Price River - Water Canyon	Book Cliffs
Cat Canyon	Delta
Deep Creek Mountains.	Ely
Old Postal Trail	Escalante
Vernon Lake	Faust
Dirty Devil River	Hanksville
Mill & Tusher Canyon	Moab
Upper Indian Creek	Moab
Behind the Rocks	Moab
Red Rock Horse Trail	Moab
Archview Trail	Moab
Millcreek Rim Trail	Moab
Onion Creek	Moab
Pack Creek Trail	Moab
Kens Lake	Moab
Harts Draw	Moab
Wheat Grass	Monte Cristo
Yellowstone Drainage	Moon Lake
Nebo Bench Trail	Nebo Loop
Maples	Ogden
Green Pond	Ogden
Cutler Basin	Ogden
Beus Canyon	Ogden
Skullcrack	Ogden
Skyline Trail	Ogden
Pioneer Trail	Ogden
Indian Trail	Ogden
Ben Lomond Peak	Ogden
Lewis Peak	Ogden
Skintoe/Baldy Peak	Ogden

Rich Trail	Panguitch
Red Canyon	Panguitch
Ledge Point	Panguitch
Casto Canyon	Panguitch
Cassidy Trail	Panguitch
Thunder Mountain	Panguitch
Barney Cove Panguitch	Panguitch
Losee Canyon	Panguitch
Millcreek Canyon	Park City
Glenwild	Park City
Blue John Canyon	Robbers Roost
Nine Mile Canyon	San Rafael
Pine Valley	St. George
Little Babylon	St. George
East Hickman	Stansbury Mountains
Front Trail	Stansbury Mountains
Rock Creek Drainage to Squaw Peak	Stillwater Dam
Cedar Mountains.	Tooele
Simpson Springs	Tooele
Hell Hole Lake	Uinta's
Red Castle	Uinta's
Bobs Lake	Uinta's
White River	Vernal

APPENDIX ONE:
USING HORSES ON UTAH'S PUBLIC LANDS:
"ON THE ROAD AGAIN. TRAVELING WITH HORSES IN UTAH"
BY STEVE GUYMAN

Horses are fascinating. Horses captivate many people, and the variety of uses for horses is an endorsement to the horse's versatility. Some horses are shown in arenas. Some horses are used for rodeo events. Some horses are used for pleasure riding along trails. Some horses pack camping or hunting supplies into wilderness areas. Some horses play polo. Some horses are used in dressage competitions. Some horses work as policemen or in search and rescue efforts. Some horses jump fences. Some horses hunt. Some horses earn their keep working on ranches. As varied as these uses are, almost every horse shares something in common—*they must be transported.*

TRAVELING INSIDE UTAH

Anytime you transport a horse within the state of Utah, you must have proof of ownership with you. This can be accomplished in a number of ways, and your local state brand inspector will provide these forms. The first is to get a "Horse Permanent Travel Permit" ($20.00; good for the life of the horse). The second is to get a "Yearly Travel Inspection" ($10.00; expires on December 31 of that year). Whenever you buy or sell a horse, you will need a "Change of Ownership" ($5.00; expires in 72 hours), which the seller should furnish to provide the buyer with "title" to the horse. If you buy a horse at an auction, the seller provides an "Auction Invoice" (good for 72 hours). A "Bill of Sale" does not prove ownership. A breed "Certificate of Registration" showing your name as the original owner (but not as transferee) will also establish ownership. No health inspections are required as long as you travel within Utah. If you are transporting horses belonging to someone else, carry written permission from the owner.

CROSSING THE STATE BORDER

To prevent the spread of diseases between states, as well as protect against the transport of stolen horses, there are a number of requirements that must be met before horses can be transported into another state. You will need an Equine Infectious Anemia Laboratory Test (Coggins) with negative results, a Certificate of Veterinary Inspection (valid for thirty days,) and proof of ownership to enter another state. You must also have the same items to return to Utah.

STOPPING AT A "PORT OF ENTRY"

The "vehicles with livestock must stop" sign at Ports of Entry applies not just to commercial haulers but to anyone transporting horses, as well as cattle, sheep, pigs, wildlife, or fish. You must first drive your truck and trailer across the scales, then go into the Department of Transportation office to complete a "Livestock and Fish Movement Report." Take your paperwork with you so you will have the certificate numbers.

So you'll know - the sign "vehicles with livestock must stop" states a federal law. Bypassing a Port of Entry subjects you to a $250.00 penalty if an enforcement officer accompanies you back to the Port. However, he can cite you where he stops you with penalty of $50.00, plus $3.00 per head.

An officer at the Port of Entry may inspect your outfit to verify your gross vehicle weight doesn't exceed the manufacture's specifications for your truck and trailer. Your gross vehicle weight shouldn't exceed the tire rating either. Exceeding either weight could result in a citation. He may also check your lights, registration, and insurance.

SUMMARY:

If you are going to transport a horse, remember– you are expected to know and comply with these regulations.

Questions should be directed to your local Utah State Brand Inspector.

Note: Montana and Wyoming do not accept Utah's Yearly Travel Permit.

Note: Coggins tests are valid for six months in California, Idaho, Montana, Nevada, Oregon, Washington, and Wyoming. They are valid for one year in Arizona, Colorado, Kansas, Nebraska, New Mexico, North Dakota, Oklahoma, South Dakota, Texas, and Utah.

"WEED-FREE HORSE FEED."

The problem;

Weeds are a subject that may not seem worth much thought when measured against the myriad activities of our daily lives. Most people think of weeds as dandelions, but the fact is thousands upon thousands acres of Utah's public lands are infested with noxious weeds.

Noxious weeds are a serious problem in the western United States, and are rapidly spreading at an estimated rate of 14 percent each year. These weeds–many of them introduced by early settlers–interfere with the growth of useful plants, clog waterways, and in some cases can even threaten the lives of animals that feed on them. Species like Leafy Spurge, Squarrose Knapweed, Russian Knapweed, Musk

Thistle, Dalmatian Toadflax, Purple Loosestrife, and many others, are alien to the United States and have no natural enemies to keep the population in balance. "Among other things, widespread infestations can lead to soil erosion and stream sedimentation," explains Larry Maxfield, Utah BLM State Office Range Conservationist. "These noxious weeds impact revegetation efforts by out-competing desirable species. They reduce wild and domestic grazing capacities, can occasionally irritate public land users by aggravating allergies, and certainly threaten our federally protected plants and animals."

The solution:

Back in 1994, to halt the spread of noxious weeds into backcountry areas, a program was started to ban the use of single ingredient feeds, which were not certified, to be free of noxious weed seeds. This program has evolved to the point where on February 11, 2003, Jack G. Troyer, the Regional Forester for the Intermountain Region of the U. S. Forest Service, signed order number 04–00–097. This prohibits possessing, storing or transporting non-palletized hay, straw, or mulch on National Forest System Lands without having each individual bale or container tagged or marked as weed free, or having original and current evidence of weed free certification documentation present.

Any violation of this prohibition is punishable by a fine of not more than $5,000.00 for an individual or $10,000 for an organization, and/or imprisonment for not more than six months.

The effect of this prohibition is horsemen (as well as hunters, woolgrowers, cattle ranchers, government trappers, conservation officers, forest rangers and anyone else who transports feed) are required to use "certified noxious weed-free feed." Utah grown feed that has been certified will have a tag attached stating the Utah Department of Agriculture and Food has inspected it. The states of Colorado, Idaho,

Nebraska, North Dakota, South Dakota, Montana, and Utah have agreed to accept each other's certification tags. Other approved products for livestock feed on public lands include pellets, hay cubes, and processed and certified hay available at some feed stores in Utah. Grains are not included in this order.

Commercially prepared feed containing more than one ingredient is defined as a "commercial feed" and falls under a different set of regulations. These feeds meet other standards and have already been inspected, so they are exempt from this Forest Service ban.

While not covered by this specific order, the ban on non-certified hay, straw, and mulch also applies to land administered by the Bureau of Land Management.

Your questions should be directed to your County Weed Supervisor or Agricultural Inspector.

THE HIGH PICKET LINE

It's up to you! There is only so much backcountry, and a growing population continues to put increasing pressure on these limited areas. It is in the interest of all those who enjoy the backcountry to impact it as little as possible. The alternative is escalating regulation and restricted use.

There is no single act that brings the horseman more poor marks or leaves a more lasting effect than tying a horse to a tree. When a horse is tied to a tree for a long time, the surrounding ground is pawed away from the roots, the tree's bark is damaged, and the adjacent ground cover is broken and torn. Manure and urine are concentrated and contaminate the immediate area.

One of the preferred methods of restraining halter broke horses is with the use of a "high picket line." This is a line, approximately seven feet above the ground, that is tightly stretched between two trees. Lead ropes are tied to the high line at the drop knots.

The high picket line prevents the horse from getting around the tree where the bark or root systems are damaged. Horses are relaxed and content when tied to a high picket line. They seldom pull against the line because there is nothing solid to pull against. With the knot above their heads, even the most skilled horses cannot untie their lead ropes or slip their halters.

Rope Selection:

The same cotton rope used to stake out a grazing horse can be converted to a high picket line. However, fifty feet of 3/8-inch multi-filament polypropylene rope makes a better choice as it is strong, light, and doesn't soak up water. Nylon is stretchy (although the braid-on-braid variety greatly overcomes this drawback) and stiffens in lower temperatures. While some horsemen use their pack lash ropes, caution should be used since a broken lash rope will cause other problems.

Location:

The high picket line should be set up away from the immediate campsite. Away from the trail and back in the trees where the least ground cover will be disturbed is the best location. Rocky soil shows less impact than softer areas.

Move the line before the trampling damage reaches the point where smoothing out the topsoil and debris doesn't erase the impact. Since one of the objectives is to protect the tree, use straps, a cinch, sacks, or stick spacers to keep the rope off the bark.

Set up:

The high picket line can be set up properly very quickly. Select a tree and wrap it with a tree saver strap approximately seven feet above the ground. Fasten one end of your picket line to the strap's D-ring with a bowline knot. String your picket line towards the other selected tree. Tie the drop knots, or insert the accessories, to which you will tie the lead ropes. Space these knots far enough apart so neighboring horses won't get tangled. Five or six feet (distance depends on rope length and stretch) from the second tree saver strap, tie a Dutchman or butterfly knot. Run the end of the picket line through the D-ring and back to the Dutchman or butterfly knot. Pulling slack between the D-ring and this knot will allow the high picket line to be pulled as tight as a fiddle string (it'll still be drooping in the morning). Get it tight–problems develop when the line gets slack.

Tying Lead Ropes:

While a lead rope can be directly tied to the high picket line, there are better methods that will prevent the lead rope from sliding along the high picket line. Drop knots can be tied with either a picket line loop or a butterfly knot. A carabineer snapped into the drop knot makes a convenient and strong connection to tie to. Tie the Dutchman or butterfly knots tightly. If there is slack, tightening the high picket line will draw the slack out of the drop knot and can bind the lead rope. The lead rope should have a swivel in it. Tie the lead rope short enough that neighboring horses can't tangle up each other. Tie it just long enough so the horse can get his head to the ground. Any longer would allow the horse to step over the lead rope and probably cause a wreck.

Summary:

The Forest Service claims 80 percent of the damage to the environment from horsemen is due to improper restraining techniques. By utilizing the high picket line, horsemen can effectively eliminate the irritant most likely to lead to restrictions in their use of the backcountry.

SUGGESTIONS FOR LOW IMPACT HORSE CAMPING

It's up to you! There is only so much "backcountry," and a growing population continues to put increasing pressure on these limited areas. It is in the interest of all those who enjoy the backcountry to impact it as little as possible.

The alternative is escalating regulation and restricted use.

Camp:

A low impact camp does not happen without planning ahead. Planning can be an enjoyable part of the trip. Take only what is required. The less you take, the fewer stock will be required. Make a neat camp and keep things together so nothing will be left behind. Many National Forests require stock groups to carry an ax, shovel, and bucket. A hand saw is handy.

Select your campsite at least two hundred feet from trails or water. Pitch your camp in an area where it will have the least visual impact. No one wants to go to the wilderness for solitude and camp within sight or sound of other people.

Conserve the site. Others will almost certainly use it. Plan ahead. Do not cut trees for picket pins, tent stakes, or ridge poles. Restrain you stock in an appropriate area. Don't set your corral in a place that someone else might choose for their camp's kitchen or bedroom. Use existing campsites if possible.

Toilet sites must also be at least two hundred feet from any water. It is better to dig a "cat hole" than a deep latrine. Make the hole no deeper than eight inches. This is where the soil breaks down waste the quickest. Be sure the toilet paper is completely buried. No one likes to come across these "tissue flowers."

Consider cooking over propane or white gas stoves in order to save firewood. Gather firewood away from the campsite. Be sure the campfire is built with an eye towards safety and visual impact. Allowing a hot fire to burn out leaves less charred wood than throwing a bucket of water on a burning fire. Be certain your fire is out when you are finished with it. Fire safety must be ingrained in every backcountry user.

Don't use nails or wire on trees, and do not leave pole corrals standing. Don't build permanent structures or caches. No one should be able to find your campsite after you leave.

Do not bury garbage. What cannot be burned must be packed out. If you packed it in—pack it out. Make an effort to preserve the backcountry by bringing any litter out with you.

Feeding stock:

Horses and mules must eat, and they do trample the grass. How much of an impact this makes depends upon the horseman. Train your horses to be hobbled and staked out. Move stakes frequently.

Many areas require that any hay or straw brought in must be certified to be weed-free. This may be difficult. A good alternative is pelletized feed. Be sure to accustom stock to pellets before the trip.

Restraining stock:

Many areas lend themselves to pole corrals. Protect the bark of trees to which you lash poles. Take the corral down before you leave.

Many horsemen are finding their stock least troublesome when held inside an electric fence. There are many portable units available. The stock must be introduced to the electric fence before the trip. Nothing causes horsemen such bad marks as tying stock to trees. Many animals will chew the bark off the tree. Inevitably, damage occurs to the root system. Use a high picket line and move it before any permanent damage occurs.

Before you leave a place, spread the manure. While moist, it is easy to break up and spread. Once dried, it is difficult to break up and becomes unsightly to many backcountry users in addition to attracting flies.

Be aware of the damage your horses may do and try to eliminate it. Keep improving your minimum impact camping techniques. While it is tough for the horse camper to leave no trace, it can be done.

Summary:

A pack trip through beautiful backcountry is a great experience. We must take care of the backcountry so future generations will be as fortunate as we to ride good horses through the same unspoiled country.

Mountain Manners:

Finally, all the planning, preparations, and travel are complete. Now you're at the trailhead ready to head into the mountains for this year's "trip of a lifetime." Riders and horses are excited and anxious to get on the trail. It seems like forever before everything is ready, and the ramrod sings "Move out!" Once in motion, it doesn't take very long for the horses and their riders to settle into a comfortable walk on the trail into the backcountry. Soon each rider is lost in his or her own thoughts as the beauty of the pristine wilderness moves by at the relaxing rhythmic beat of horse's hooves. What could be better? A trip into beautiful backcountry is a fantastic experience. Other people also enjoy this same experience but may travel differently than horsemen. With the limited amount of backcountry available, it is inevitable those who use it will come into more and more contact with each other. This contact need not cause conflict. To avoid regulation and restricted use, it is in the interest of all those who enjoy the backcountry to have good mountain manners. Courtesy and common sense will resolve any situation.

Your string of horses on the trail:

Avoid surprises while on the trail. Designate a rider to ride "point" about thirty yards ahead of the pack string. This rider will be alert to overtaking or meeting other groups. Obstacles will be evaluated and the rest of the group advised. The pack string comes next. Put a rider on "drag" behind the string to watch the packs. The rider should be alert to anything dropped on the trail and watch for other parties overtaking the pack string.

Other pack strings:

When two pack strings meet head on, usually the more maneuverable of the strings is the one that yields the trail. When large pack strings meet along a steep, narrow grade, it is traditional for the string going uphill to have the trail right-of-way. The rules of reason and common sense should prevail.

Pedestrians:

Many horses are not familiar with the profile backpackers present. The point rider should explain this to the hikers and, since they are usually more maneuverable, politely ask them to step off the trail far enough to the downhill side to let the horses pass. Advising the hikers to speak to the passing stock will assure the horses there is no danger. Occasionally you'll meet hikers leading llamas. Although many horses have not been introduced to llamas, this may not be the best time or place. The most maneuverable party should yield the trail. Courtesy and common sense will resolve this situation.

Bicycles:

The speed and quietness of bicycles create the major hazards to an encounter. The point or drag riders should politely ask the bikers to stop, move to the side, and talk to the horses as they pass. All riders should thank the bikers for their courtesy.

Vehicles:

ATVs, motorcycles, jeeps and trucks, while limited where they may travel, are none the less encountered off roads. The point or drag rider must advise the other riders of the oncoming traffic and make himself visible to the vehicle's driver. Most states require drivers to obey hand signals given by a mounted horseman–but don't count on it! It is best to get completely off the track and let them slowly pass.

Summary:

We must take care of the backcountry so future generations will be as fortunate as we to ride good horses through the same unspoiled country. Since others use this same country, we will all have to get along. No rules will ever replace courtesy and good manners.

RULES FOR VISITORS TO UTAH'S PUBLIC LANDS

Living in the West, horsemen are very fortunate to have access to so much public land. Whether the land is administered by the USDA Forest Service, the National Park Service, the U.S. Fish & Wildlife Service, Utah State Parks & Recreation, the Utah Department of Wildlife Resources, the Bureau of Land Management, or the Bureau of Reclamation, today's Utah horsemen can pretty much ride where they want relatively unencumbered by prohibitive regulations.

Part of the Backcountry Horsemen of America's purpose is to perpetuate our heritage of common sense use and enjoyment of horses in America's backcountry. One of the strategies to accomplish this goal is to avoid creating situations where regulations become necessary. As a visitor to Utah's public lands, you are asked to follow certain rules designed to protect the land, the natural environment, to ensure the health and safety of others, and to promote pleasant and rewarding outdoor recreation experiences for all visitors.

Campfires

- Obey restrictions on fires. Open fires may be limited or prohibited at certain times.
- Within campgrounds and other established sites, build fires only in fire rings, stoves, grills, or fireplaces provided for this purpose.
- Be sure your fire is completely extinguished before leaving. You are responsible for keeping fires under control!

Property

- Do not carve, chop, cut, or damage any live trees. Do not drive nails or stick an axe into live trees.
- Leave natural areas the way you found them.
- Enter buildings, structures, or enclosed areas only

when they are expressly open to the public.

- Native American, old cabins, and other structures, along with objects and artifacts associated with them, have historic or archeological value. Do not damage or remove any such historic or archeological resource.

Sanitation

- Throw all garbage and litter into containers provided for this purpose, or take it with you. "Pack it in—pack it out." Show our concern for the public lands by cleaning up after others.
- Wash food and personal items away from drinking water supplies. Use water faucets only for drawing water.
- Prevent pollution—keep garbage, litter, and foreign substances out of lakes, streams ,and other water.
- Use toilets properly. Do not throw garbage, litter, fish cleanings, or other foreign substances into toilets and plumbing fixtures.

Operation of Vehicles

- Obey all traffic signs. State traffic laws apply to all public lands (unless otherwise posted).
- When operating vehicles of any kind, do not damage the land or vegetation or disturb wildlife. Avoid driving on unpaved roads or trails when they are wet or muddy.

Pets

- Pets must be restrained or on a leash while in developed recreation sites.

Fireworks and Firearms

- Fireworks and explosives are prohibited on public lands.

- Firing a gun is not allowed: a) in or within 150 yards of a residence, building, campsite, developed recreation site or occupied area; b) across or on a road or body of water; and c) in any circumstance whereby a person may be injured or property damaged.

Horses

- Saddle or pack animals are allowed within recreation sites only where authorized by posted instructions.
- Stay on trails. Cutting across switchbacks damages the trails, vegetation, and our image.
- Scatter all manure. Scattered manure is fertilizer, but manure piles are offensive to non-horsemen. Don't scrape fertilizer out of your trailer, and pick up manure that falls out while unloading and loading.
- Feed stock only weed-free hay (and straw) or commercially prepared pellets while on public lands. Besides avoiding fines, we avoid introducing noxious weeds into the very backcountry we're trying to preserve.
- Do not tie horses to trees. Nothing gives horsemen poorer marks than trees killed by horses pawing the dirt to expose the roots or chewing the bark. Use a high picket line—your horses (and the public) will thank you for it.
- Be courteous on the trail. Although regulations are posted as to who has the right-of-way on the trail, nothing works like courtesy.

Most public lands have unique and interesting attractions and are managed for visitors to enjoy. If all visitors use common sense and courtesy, these attractions will be there for many future generations to enjoy.

Lead the way—show others how much horsemen value Utah's public lands!

APPENDIX TWO:
USGS 1:24,000 MAPS AND
MAP NUMBERS:

Antelope Island N, # 41112-A2-TF-024
Birdseye, #39111-H5-TF-024
Bottle Neck Peak, #39110-A6-TF-024
Bountiful Peak, USGF # 40111-H7-TF-024
Bridal Veil Falls, # 4011-C5-TF-024
Bull Valley Gorge, #37112-D1-TF-024
Christmas Meadow, # 40110-G7-TF-0224
Coalville, Wanship, Park City East, Park City West
Deseret Peak East, # 40112-D5-TF-024
Devils Slide, #41111-A5-TF-024
Dewey - #38109-G3TF-024
Draper, # 40111-E7-TF-024
Dromedary Peak, 40111-E6-TF-024
Erickson Basin, # 40111-F1-TF-024
Erickson Basin, # 40111-F1-TF-0242
Hayden Peak, # 40110-F7-TF-024
Hoyt Peak, # 40111-F2-TF-024
Jordan Narrows 40111-D8-TF-024
Lehi, #40111-D7-TF-024
Midvale, USGF #40111-E8-TF-024
Mirror Lake, #40110-F8-TF-024
Orem, # 40111-C6-TF-024
Payson Lakes, # 39111-H6-TF-024
Red Knob, # 40110-G6-TF-024
Rill Creek, # 38109-E4-TF-024
Slickrock Bench, #37111-D8-TF-024
Springville - # 40111-B5-TF-024

Steele Butte, #38110-A8-TF-024
Strawberry Res. SE, # 40111-A1-TF-024
Sugar Loaf Butte, #38110-D2-TF-024
The Post, #37110-G8-TF024
Timpanogas Cave, # 40111-D6-TF-024
Veyo, #37113-C6-TF-024

APPENDIX THREE:
VETERINARIANS LISTED BY CITY

American Fork Veterinary Clinic, 1086 S 860 E, American Fork (801) 756–3990

Country View Veterinary Hospital, 582 Pacific Dr, American Fork (801) 763–1900

Indian Creek Veterinary Clinic, 1501 N Highway 357, Beaver (435) 438–2873

Blue Mountain Veterinary SVC, 1000 E Browns Canyon # 103–14, Blanding (435) 678–2414

Animal Emergency Clinic, 463 W 500 S, Bountiful (801) 292–8228

Animal Medical Clinic, 215 S 500 W, Bountiful, (801) 292–7219

Bear River Animal Hospital, 88 S 950 W, Brigham City (435) 734–9831

Brigham City Animal Hospital, 852 N Main St, Brigham City (435) 723–8248

Cedar Veterinary Clinic, 533 N Airport Rd, Cedar City (435) 586–3400

Mountain View Animal Clinic, 2265 W Midvalley Rd, Cedar City (435) 586–4918

Southern Utah Animal Hospital, 1203 N Main St, Cedar City (435) 586–6216

Parrish Creek Veterinary Clinic, 24 W Parrish Lane, Centerville (801) 298–2014

A Animal Hospital, 1499 State St, Clearfield (801) 776–4507

Clearfield Veterinary Clinic, 428 N Main St, Clearfield (801) 776–4372

Great Basin Veterinary SVC, 1115 E Main St, Delta (435) 864–3921

Dr. Buzz Marden, Po Box 1222, Draper (801) 572–1456

Meadowlands Veterinary Hospital, 12444 S 300 E, Draper (801) 572–5403

Bear River Veterinary Clinic, 619 Almy Rd. #107, Evanston, WY (307) 789–5230

R J White, 879 Shepard Lane, Farmington, (801) 451–2359

Gunnison Valley Animal Clinic, 630 S Main, Gunnison (435) 528–7900

Arcadia Veterinary Clinic, 90 E 1520 Highway 40 N, Heber City (435) 654–0592

Isom P. Wade, 899 W. 100 S., Heber, 84032, (435)654–3500

Wasatch Animal Hospital, 31 W Center St, Heber City (435) 654–3837

Holladay Veterinary Clinic, 4647 S 2300 E, Holladay (801) 278–2859

Randazzo Animal Health Care, 4038 S 2700 E, Holladay (801) 278–9494

Valley Veterinary Clinic, 10010 E 200 S, Huntsville (801) 745–2697

Desert Vet, 470 W State St, Hurricane, (435) 635–7000

Hurricane Animal Hospital, 1545 W Highway 9, Hurricane (435) 635–7387

Virgin River Veterinary Clinic, 525 W State St, Hurricane (435) 635–4161

Hyrum Small Animal Clinic, 425 S Center St, Hyrum (435) 245–4111

Kanab Veterinary Hospital, 484 S 100 E, Kanab (435) 644–2400

Fairfield Veterinary Hospital, 230 N Fairfield Rd, Layton (801) 544–8800

Kay's Creek Veterinary Clinic, 1010 S Angel St, Layton (801) 544–3552

Layton Veterinary Hospital, 1538 N Main St, Layton (801) 773–2570

Utah Veterinary Specialists, 1095 N Main St, Layton (801) 497–9225

Bridgerland-Cache Animal Hosp, 95 W 900 N, Logan (435) 752–2151

Cache Meadow Veterinary Clinic, 38 E 2600 N, Logan (435) 752–6135

Mountain View Veterinary Clinic, 1702 N 800 E, Logan (435) 752–8251

Moab Veterinary Clinic, 4575 Spanish Valley Dr, Moab (435) 259–8710

River Valley Vet Hospital, 395 N 400 E, Morgan, (801) 829–3632

David P Nicholson, 4200 S State, Mt Carmel (435) 648–2010

Mountain Vale Veterinary Clinic, 1114 W 4800 S, Murray (801) 266–1701

Redwood Veterinary Hospital, 4958 S Redwood Rd, Murray (801) 966–3974

Salt Creek Veterinary SVC, 34 N Main St, Nephi (435) 623–5405

Ben Lomond Animal Clinic, 1380 N Highway 91, Ogden (801) 782–9679

Brookside Animal Hospital, 138 W 12th St, Ogden (801) 399–5897

Burch Creek Animal Hospital, 4847 Harrison Blvd, Ogden (801) 479–4410

Central Weber Animal Hospital, 1689 W 2550 S, Ogden (801) 394–4208

Erz Animal Hospital, 5585 Harrison Blvd, Ogden (801) 479–3158

Golden Spike Equine Hospital, 1367 W 400 N, Ogden (801) 399–2460

Johnston Animal Hospital, 2454 Monroe Blvd, Ogden (801) 393–7387

Mountain States Equine, 7283 W 900 S, Ogden (801) 731–4244

North Ogden Animal Hospital, 1580 N Washington Blvd, Ogden (801) 782–4401

Ogden Animal Hospital, 208 Washington Blvd, Ogden (801) 392–0633

Animal Clinic, 1425 S State St, Orem (801) 225–0774

Animal Medical SVC, 469 W Center St, Orem, (801) 225–3346

Ribbonwood Animal Hospital, 559 W 1830 N, Orem (801) 226–0168

Utah Valley Veterinary Hosp, 525 S State St, Orem (801) 225–5395

Blacksmith Fork Vet Clinic, 10687 S Highway 165, Paradise (435) 245–4710

Park City Animal Clinic, 1950 Woodbine Way # 10, Park City (435) 649–0710

White Pine Veterinary Clinic, 2100 Rasmussen Rd, Park City (435) 649–7182

C Wright, 1950 Woodbine Way, Park City, (435) 649–6273

West Mountain Veterinary Hospital, 143 W. 900 N. Payson, (435) 465–4648

Payson Veterinary Clinic, 765 E 100 N # 3, Payson (801) 465–4169

Rocky Mountain Large Animal Hosp, 1299 W State Rd, Pleasant Grove (801) 785–7777

Timpanogos Animal Hospital, 1299 W State Rd, Pleasant Grove (801) 785–3583

Animal Hospital, 1989 Airport Rd, Price (435) 637–5797

Castle Valley Veterinary Clinic, 1711 S Highway 10, Price (435) 637–4272

At Your Door Veterinary SVC, 164 W 580 S, Providence, (435) 753–7507

Alpine Animal Hospital, 1615 S State St, Provo (801) 374–0622

University Veterinary Clinic, 3820 N University Ave, Provo (801) 224–2233

Richfield Veterinary Clinic, 910 E 300 N, Richfield (435) 896–8606

Sevier Valley Animal Clinic, 820 S 400 W, Richfield, (435) 896–4421

North Cache Veterinary SVC, 191 W 100 N, Richmond (435) 258–2190

Valley Veterinary SVC, 715 S 250 E, Richmond (435) 258–2484

Linford Equine Practice, Riverton (801) 446–8838

Riverton Veterinary Clinic, 12619 S Redwood Rd, Riverton (801) 254–6621

Stone Ridge Large Animal Clinic, 11840 S 1381 W, Riverton (801) 254–4840

Basin Veterinary Clinic. 540 W Us Highway 40, Roosevelt (435) 722–2062

Uinta Veterinary SVC, 331 N Nelson Ave # 60–4, Roosevelt (435) 722–9066

Animal Care Roy Veterinary, 1787 Riverdale Rd., Roy (801) 825–9701

Associated Veterinarians, 5220 S 3500 W, Roy (801) 773–5617

Millcreek Veterinary Clinic, 2361 E 3300 S, Salt Lake City (801) 487–7791

South Valley Large Animal Clinic, 1791 W 11400 S, South Jordan (801) 254–2333

James A Eaton, 845 N 300 W, Spanish Fork, (801) 798–7493

Equine Medical SVC, 1101 E 800 N, Spanish Fork (801) 798–1000

Nebo Animal Clinic Inc, 845 N 300 W, Spanish Fork (801) 798–7493

Sanpete Veterinary SVC, 920 N 400 E, Spring City (435) 462–2903

Mountain West Animal Hospital, 410 S 450 W, Springville (801) 489–9676

AAA St George Veterinary, 775 S Main St, St George (435) 673–9673

Animal Clinic Of St George, 857 E Tabernacle St, St George (435) 673–9696

Animal Medical Hospital, 55 S Bluff St, St George (435) 628–1634

Brinkerhoff Large Animal Clinic, 1690 E 2450 S, St George (435) 628–3022

Dixie Veterinary Clinic, 730 N Dixie Dr, St George (435) 628–6532

Sunset Boulevard Veterinary, W Sunset Blvd, St George (435) 628–8183

Countryside Animal Clinic, 254 Main St, Tooele (435) 882–4100

Tooele Veterinary Clinic, 1182 N 80 E # 1, Tooele (435) 882–1051

Tri County Veterinary Hospital, 352 E 200 N, Torrey (435) 425–3487

Bear River Animal Hospital, 390 W 600 N, Tremonton (435) 257–7455

Ashley Valley Veterinary, 85 E 650 N, Vernal (435) 789–3022

Countryside Veterinary Clinic, 1751 S Vernal Ave, Vernal (435) 789–6697

A Visiting Veterinarian, 479 E Wendover Blvd, Wendover (435) 665–7704

SHERIFFS LISTED BY COUNTY

BEAVER COUNTY SHERIFF, 40 South 100 East P.O. Box 91Beaver, 84713 (435)438–2862

BOX ELDER COUNTY SHERIFF, 52 South 100 West Suite A, Brigham City, 84302, (435) 734–3800

CACHE COUNTY SHERIFF, 50 West 200 North Logan, 84321 (435)752–4103

CARBON COUNTY SHERIFF, 240 West Main, Price, 84501 (435)637–1622

DAGGETT COUNTY SHERIFF, 95 North 100 West, Manila, 84044 (435)784–3255

DAVIS COUNTY SHERIFF, 800 West State St., Farmington, 84025 (801)451–4120

DUCHESNE COUNTY SHERIFF, P.O. Box 985, Duchesane, 84021 (435)738–2015

EMERY COUNTY SHERIFF, P.O. Box 514 Castle Dale, 84513 (435)381–2404

GARFIELD COUNTY SHERIFF, 45 South Main, Panguitch, 84759 (435)676–2678

GRAND COUNTY SHERIFF, 125 East Center, Moab, 84532 (435)259–8115

IRON COUNTY SHERIFF, 2132 North Main St., Cedar City, 84720 (435)586–6511

JUAB COUNTY SHERIFF, 425 West Sheep lane Dr., Nephi, 84643 (435)623–1349

KANE COUNTY SHERIFF, 76 North Main, Kanab, 84741 (435)644–2349

MILLARD COUNTY SHERIFF, 765 South HWY 99 State Route, Box 50, Fillmore, 84630 (435)743–5302

MORGAN COUNTY SHERIFF, 48 West Young St, P.O. Box 1047, Morgan, 84050 (435)829–0590

PIUTE COUNTY SHERIFF, 55 North Main, Junction, 84740 (435)577–2893

RICH COUNTY SHERIFF,20 South Main St., P.0. Box 38 Randolph, 84064 (435)793–2285

SALT LAKE COUNTY SHERIFF, 2001 South State St., Salt Lake City, 84190 (801)468–3931

SAN JUAN COUNTY SHERIFF, 297 South Main St., P.O. Box 788,Monticello, 84535 (435)587–2237

SANPETE COUNTY SHERIFF, 160 North Main Street, Manti, 84442 (435)835–2191

SEVIER COUNTY SHERIFF, 835 East 300 North, #200, Richfield, 84701 (435)896–2600

SUMMIT COUNTY SHERIFF, 6300 Silver Creek Drive, Park City, 84098 Sheriff: (435)615–3500

TOOELE COUNTY SHERIFF, 47 South Main Tooele, 84074 (435)882–5600

UINTAH COUNTY SHERIFF, 152 East 100, North Vernal, 84078 (435)789–2511

UTAH COUNTY SHERIFF, P.O. Box 1547, Provo, 84603 (801)343–4001

WASATCH COUNTY SHERIFF, 1361 South Highway 40,Heber City, 84032 (435)654–9975

WASHINGTON COUNTY SHERIFF,750 South 5400 West, Hurricane, 84737 (435)656–6601

WAYNE COUNTY SHERIFF, Wayne County Courthouse, Loa, 84747 (435)836–2789

WEBER COUNTY SHERIFF, 457 26th Street, Ogden, 84401 (801)399–8183

Mountain View Sheriff, 77 County Rd. 109, Evanston, WY (307) 782–3682

Sandy Police Dept. 142 S. Main St. Sandy, (801) 255–8914

APPENDIX FIVE:
UTAH FEED AND TACK STORES

Lazy SB Leather & Saddlery, Fort Bridger, WY 82933 (307) 782–7300

K C Feeds, PO Box 246, Bear River City, 84301, 435–279–8677

Smith Feed & Garden Center, 85 N 200 W, Bountiful, 801–295–2319

Farmers Corner, 308 S Main St, Brigham City, 84302–2533, 435–734–2020

Walton Feed West Inc, Brigham City, PO Box 52, 84302–0052, 435–563–5301

Overson's Farm Center, Cedar City, 84721–0426, 435–586–4469

Wildfire Stables, 4936W 1275S, Cedar City, 84720, 435–586–4443

Alfred Fullmer Feed Store, PO Box 204, Circleville, 84723–0204, 435–577–2945

Harris Farm & Garden Supply, 2056 N 2000 W, Clearfield, 84015–8334, 801–825–7493

Hi-Valley Feed, 55 W Center St, Coalville,435–336–2517

Bear River Valley Co-op, Corinne, 435–744–2211

Bear River Fertilizer Co., Garland, 435–257–3341

Big Five Commodities, PO Box 608, Delta, 84624–0608, 435–864–2926

Big J Enterprises, 360 N 400 W, Delta, 84624–9482, 435–864–2804

Eades Commodities Co., 279 S 500 W, Delta, 84624–9268, 435–864–1888

Great Basin Feed & Supply Co, 62 N 200 E, Delta, 84624–9456, 435–864–5588

Intermountain Farmers Assn, 498 W Main St, Delta, 84624–9258, 435–864–2110

Paramount Hay Cubes, 2013 S. 4000 W, Delta, 84624, 435–864–2816

Sam Alfalfa Inc, 990 N 500 W, Delta, 84624–8762, 435–864–3031

Sugarville Cubing Co, 5626 N 3000 W, Delta, 84624–7050, 435–864–4828

Sugarville Feeders, 1885 W Ashby Rd, Delta, 84624–7357, 435–864–3821

Intermountain Farmers Assn, PO Box 907, Draper, 84020–0907, 801–571–0125

Feed Store, PO Box 357, Duchesne, 84021–0357, 801–738–2358

Evergreen Seed & Supply, 1175 N 5900 E, Eden, 84310–9724, 801–745–6643

Peterson Machine & Supply, 175 W 200 S, Fillmore, 84631–0247, 435–743–6866

Bear River Fertilizer Co., PO Box 69, Garland, 84312–0069, 435–257–3341

Hermansen Roller Mill, 204 S 100 E, Gunnison, 84634–0250, 435–528–3136

Intermountain Farmers Assn., 521 W, 200 N. Highland 84003 (801) 756–9604

Dallas Green Farm, 3752 S 4700 W, Hooper, 84315–9618, 801–731–0331

S Bar S Saddle, Tack & Western Wear, 54 N. Main St. Kamas, (435)783–4217

Intermountain Farmers Assn, 825 E Hwy 193, Layton, 84041–8648, 801–771–4989

Layton Farm Supply, 164 S Main St, Layton, 84041–3725, 801–544–5944

Loa Builders Supply, 137 N Main, Loa, 435–836–2751
   CAL Ranch Stores, 1224 N Main St, Logan, 435–753–0811

Fur Breeders Agri Co-op Assn, 1000 W 200 N, Logan, 84321–8255, 435–752–5441

Trenton Feed Co-op, 280 W 300 S, Logan, 84321–5215, 435–753–0181

Ball Feed & Horse Supply, 7490 S Holden ST, Midvale, 801–255–2621

Minersville Feed & Supply, 88 E, 100 S, Minersville, 435–386–2222

Spanish Valley Feed Store, 2728 S Hwy 191, Moab, 84532–3443, 435–259–6315

Alpine Clean Foods, 15750 N 3000 E, Moroni, 84646, 435–436–8218

Moroni Feed Co., PO Box 368, Moroni, 84646–0368, 435–436–8221

Dee's Tire & Farm Supply, 1845 S Morgan Valley Dr, Morgan, 84050–9673, 801–829–6523

Ross Brothers Feed & Seed, Myton, 84052–0147, 435–722–3441

Greenline, 795 S Main, Nephi, 435–623–1358

Cache Commodities, PO Box 387, Ogden, 84402–0387, 801–392–2490

CNR Country Feed & Pet, 795 W 24th St, Ogden, 801–393–3700

Farr West Farm & Feed, 897 N 2000 W, Ogden, 84404–9425, 801–731–2745

Panguitch Supply, 700 N Main, Panguitch, 435–676–2232

Equus Equestrian Tack, 6400 N Pace Front Rd, Park City, 435–615–7433

Broken Spoke Tack Shop, 898 E. 100 N. Payson, (801) 756–9604

Intermountain Farmers Assoc, 444 E 100 N, Payson, 84651–2340, 801–465–4815

Intermountain Farmers Assn, 55 W 500 S, Provo, 84601–
4527, 801–373–7680

Diamond W Imp, 10 N Main, Randolph, 435–793–2725

Anderson's Quarter Horse & Tack, 635 S State, Redmond,
435–529–7328

Intermountain Farmers Assn, 1860 W 12600 S, Riverton,
84065–7026, 801–254–3501

Buchanan Feed Corp, 278 E 100 N, Roosevelt, 84066–
3008, 435–722–3905

Intermountain Farmers Assn, Salt Lake City, 84130–0168,
801–972–3009

Saddle Up, 11415 S. Redwood Road, So. Jordan, 84095
(801) 294–5700

Burns Saddlery Inc., 79 W. Main St. Salina, (435) 529–
7484

Holyoak Saddles, 287 N. Bluff, St. George, (435) 673–
9548

CAL Ranch Stores, 950 N Main St, 801 Spanish Fork, -
794–2810

Intermountain Farmers Assn, 250 Arrowhead Trail Rd,
Spanish Fork, 84660–9232, 801–798–7418

Leland Milling Co, 905 S Mill Rd, Spanish Fork, 84660,
801–798–2090

R C's Horse Supply, 490 W 300 N, Smithfield, 84335–1820,
435–563–5682

Winn Inc, PO Box 332, Smithfield, 84335–0332, 435–563–
6215

Trenton Feed Co-op, 235 W Main St, Trenton, 84338–9634,
435–563–6204

Venice feed & Cattle Co, 446 N Main, Venice, 435–896–
5260

Ponderosa Feed, 1297 W 625 S, Vernal, 435–789–0125

S & S Barns and Buildings Inc, West Jordan, 5476 West
Wells Park Rd, 801–282–1834

AA Callister Corp, 3615 S Redwood Rd, West Valley City,

84119, 801–973–7058

JS2 Tack & Saddlery, 759 Main Wellington (435) 737–4428

APPENDIX SIX:
PUBLIC LAND AGENCIES
USDA Forest Service

Intermountain Region, 324 25th St., Ogden, 84401, (801) 625–5182

Forest Service Information Office, 2501 Wall Ave. Ogden, 84403, (801) 625–5306

Wasatch–Cache, 125 South State Street, Salt Lake City, 84138, (801) 236–3400

- **Logan Ranger District,** 1500 East Highway 89, Logan, 84327, (435) 755–3620
- **Ogden Ranger District,** 507 25th Street, Ogden, 84403, (801) 625–5112
- **Salt Lake Ranger District,** 6944 South 3000 East, Salt Lake City, 84121, (801) 733–2660
- **Evanston Ranger District,** 1565 Highway 150, Suite A, P.O. Box 1880, Evanston, WY 82930 (307) 789–3194
- **Mountain View Ranger District,** P.O. Box 129, Mountain View, WY 82939, (307) 782–6555
- **Kamas Ranger District,** 50 East Center Street, Kamas, 84036, (435) 783–4338

Dixie National Forest, 1789 Wedgewood Lane, Cedar City, 84720, (435) 865–3700

- **Pine Valley Ranger District,** 345 E. Riverside Drive, St. George, 84771 (435)652–3100
- **Cedar City Ranger District,** 1789 Wedgewood Lane, Cedar City, 84720, (435) 865–3200
- **Powell Ranger District,** P.O. Box 80, Panguitch,

84759–0080, (435) 676–9300
- **Escalante Ranger District,** P.O. Box 246, Escalante, 84726–0246, (435) 826–5400
- **Teasdale Ranger District,** P.O. Box 90, Teasdale, 84773–0090, (435) 425–9500

Ashley National Forest, 355 North Vernal Ave., Vernal, 84078, (435) 789–1181
- **Duchesne/Roosevelt Ranger District Duchesne Office,** 85 West Main , P.O. Box 981, Duchesne, 84021, (435)738–2482
- **Duchesne/Roosevelt Ranger District Roosevelt Office,** 650 W Highway 40,Box 127, Roosevelt, 84066, 435–722–5018
- **Vernal Ranger District,** 355 North Vernal Avenue, Vernal, 84078, (435)789–1181
- **Flaming Gorge Ranger District,** 25 West Highway 43, P.O. Box 279, Manila, 84046 435–784–3445

Fishlake National Forest, 115 E 900 N, Richfield, 84701, (435) 896–9233
- **Fillmore Ranger District,** 390 S. Main, Fillmore, 84631, (435)743–5721
- **Loa Ranger District,** 138 S. Main, Loa, 84747, (435) 836–2811
- **Beaver Ranger District,** 575 S. Main, Beaver, 84713, (435) 438–2436Richfield Ranger District, 115 E. 900 N. Richfield, 84701, (435) 896–9233

Manti-La Sal National Forest, 599 W. Price River Dr., Price, 84501, (435) 637–2817
- **Sanpete Ranger District,** 540 N. Main, Ephraim, 84627, (435) 283–4151
- **Ferron Ranger District,** 115 W. Canyon RD., Ferron,

84523, (435) 384–2372
- **Moab Ranger District,** 2290 S. West Resource Blvd., Moab, 84532, (435) 259–7155

Uinta National Forest, 88 West 100 North, Provo, 84601, (801) 342–5100
- **Spanish Fork Ranger District,** 44 West 400 North, Spanish Fork, 84660, (801) 798–3571
- **Pleasant Grove Ranger District,** 390 North 100 East, Pleasant Grove, 84062, (801) 785–3563
- **Spanish Fork Ranger District,** 635 North Main, Nephi, 84648, (435) 623–2735
- **Heber Ranger District,** 2460 South Highway 40, PO Box 190, Heber City, 84032 (435) 654–0470

State of Utah Land Management Offices
Division of Wildlife Resources, 1594 West North Temple, Suite 2110, Salt Lake City, 84114–6480 **(801) 538–4700**
Division of Forestry, Fire & State Lands, 1594 West North Temple, Suite 3520Salt Lake City, 84114–6480, **(801) 538–5555**
Division of State Parks & Recreation, 1594 West North Temple, Suite 116, Salt Lake City, 84114–6480, **(801) 538–7220**
- **Antelope Island State Park,** 4528 W 1700 South Syracuse Entrance Station, (801) 773–2941
- **Historic Union Pacific Rail Trail State Park,** P.O. Box 754, Park City, 84060–0754, (435–649–6839)

Bureau of Land Management

Utah State Office, 324 S, State, Suite 301, Salt Lake City, 84111, (801)539–40001

Salt Lake District, 2370 S. 2300 W. Salt Lake City, 84119, (801) 977–4300

Cedar City District, 176 E. D.L. Sergeant Drive, Cedar City, (435) 586–2401

Richfield District, 150 E. 900 N. Richfield, 84701, (435) 869–8221

Moab District, 82 E. Dogwood, Moab 84532, (435) 259–6111

Vernal District, 170 S. 500 E., Vernal, 84078, (435) 781–4400

Grand Staircase-Escalante National Monument, 337 S. Main St. Cedar City, 84720 (435) 865–9214

National Parks

Capital Reef National Park, HC 70 Box 15, Torrey, 84775 (435) 425–3791

Canyon Lands National Park, 2282 SW Resource Blvd, Moab, 84532, (435)719–2313

City and County Offices

Bluffdale City, 14175 South Redwood Road, Bluffdale, 84065, (801) 254–2200

Draper City Offices, 12441 S. 900 E., Draper, 84020, (801)576–6500

Salt Lake County Parks and Rec. Adm., 2001 South State Street S4400, Salt Lake City, 84190, (801)483–5473

APPENDIX SEVEN:
HOSPITALS AND MEDICAL CENTERS

Utah Valley Regional MED Center, 1034 N 500 W, Provo, 84604, (801) 357–7056

Alta View Hospital, 9660 S 1300 E, Sandy, 84094, (801) 501–2600

Heber Valley Medical Center, 1485 South Highway 40, HEBER CITY, (435) 654–2500

Mountain West Medical Center, 2055 N Main, TOOELE, (435) 843–3600

Jordan Valley Hospital, 3580 W. 9000 S., West Jordan, (801) 561–8888

Evanston Regional Hospital, 190 Arrowhead Dr, Evanston, WY 82930 - 9266, (307) 789–3636

South Davis Community Hospital, 401 S 400 E, Bountiful, 84010, (801) 295–2361

Castle View Hospital, 300 N. Hospital Dr., Price, 84501, (435) 637–4800

Fillmore Community Medical Center, 674 S. Hwy. 99, Fillmore, 84631, (435) 676–8811

IHC (Richfield), 1000 N. Main, Venice, 84701, (435) 896–8271

Green River Medical Center, 305 W. Main, Green River, (435) 564–3434

MaKay-Dee Hospital, 4401 Harrison Boulevard, Ogden, 84403, 801–627–2800

River Road IHC Health Center, 577 S. River Road, St. George, 84790, (435) 688–6100

Springville IHC Health Center, 385 S. 400 E., Springville, 84663, (801) 489–3244

Sevier Valley Hospital IHC, 1100 N. Main, Richfield, (435)

896–8271

Allen Memorial Hospital, 719 West Fourth Street, Moab,
Tel.1–435–259–7191

Logan Regional Hospital, 1400 N. 500 E., Logan, Utah
(435) 716–4000

HAPPY TRAILS!

NOTES

274

Contact Bruce Kartchner
or order more copies of this book at

TATE PUBLISHING, LLC

127 East Trade Center Terrace
Mustang, Oklahoma 73064

(888) 361 - 9473

Tate Publishing, LLC

www.tatepublishing.com